*Discovering The Details of
Familiar New Testament Passages*

BY JENNIFER DEVLIN

114 Bush Rd | Nashville, TN 37217
randallhouse.com

Verses We Know By Heart

© 2009 by Jennifer Devlin

Published by Randall House
114 Bush Road
Nashville, TN 37217

All rights reserved. No part of this publication may be reproduced, stored in a retrieval system, or transmitted in any form or by any means—electronic, mechanical, photocopy, recording, or any other means—except for brief quotation in critical reviews, without the prior permission of the publisher.

All Scripture quotations, unless otherwise indicated, are taken from the New American Standard Bible (NASB) © 1960, 1962, 1963, 1968, 1971, 1972, 1973, 1975 1977, 1995 by the Lockman Foundation. (www.Lockman.org). Used by permission. Scripture quotations marked HCSB are taken from the Holman Christian Standard Bible®, Copyright © 1999, 2000, 2002, 2003 by Holman Bible Publishers. Used by permission. Holman Christian Standard Bible®, Holman CSB®, and HCSB® are federally registered trademarks of Holman Bible Publishers.

Printed in the United States of America

10-ISBN 0892655542

13-ISBN 9780892655540

www.randallhouse.com

To the friends God has brought along side me in this journey. You have spurred me on in my desire to get women excited about the Word of God, and I thank you!

CONTENTS

Introduction iv

Week 1 The Miraculous Love of God – John 3:1–21 1

Week 2 Connecting to the Savior – Romans 8:26–39 23

Week 3 Blessed as a Believer – Matthew 5:1-12 45

Week 4 Seeking the Lord – Matthew 6:5-13 69

Week 5 The True Meaning of Love – 1 Corinthians 12:31 - 13:13 91

Week 6 Making the Perfect Fruit Salad – Galatians 5:16-26 111

Note to Leaders 132

INTRODUCTION

Hey, friend!

I'm honored to have you joining me on this trek through the *Verses We Know by Heart*. In our fast paced world, it's easy to get caught up in a drive-by approach to Scripture study. During the next six chapters together, we'll take some time to dig into familiar passages, learning more about the context and life application principles of some of the most pivotal concepts of Christianity. I'm a firm believer that God has given us His Word in order to reveal who Jesus is and why He has come to save us, as well as to teach us how we can live powerful, transformed lives. But to implement His Word, we first need to understand it. That's where this study series comes in.

If you've completed the first study in this series, *Verses We Know by Heart: Discovering the Details of Familiar Old Testament Passages,* you've already found out that there's much more to the passages of the Old Testament than our bumper stickers and t-shirts can display. You've built a firm foundation on details about creation, the Law, God's wisdom, and so much more. I thank you for continuing this journey of discovery with another look at some of our sound-byte favorites.

If this is your first time looking at the *Verses We Know by Heart series,* welcome! This study can be completed individually or in a small group setting. If your church doesn't have a small group option for women, I challenge you to start one. Not able to meet at church? Consider meeting in your living room or at your kitchen table, or during your lunch break at work. Find a few friends and dive into this guide together. Tap into the supplemental leader resources we're providing, available at www.randallhouse.com, and go for it. Brew a pot of coffee to share, and have some fun. Let God knit your hearts together through His Word.

I'm a living testament to the power of small group discipleship—the Lord used a women's Bible study class to draw me to Jesus, and it was there that I fell in love with Him and His Word and began applying biblical truths to my broken life. Together, you and your small group can encourage each other along the road of spiritual growth, learning from each other and the precepts tucked into our focus passages.

As I have written this book I've been praying for you. I have been praying that you will fall head over heels in love with your Savior and be transformed by His love, displaying that discovery in your actions, interactions, and life.

Growing in the love of Jesus with you,

Jennifer

WEEK ONE

The Miraculous Love of God

Embracing the Savior

John 3:1–21

Do you remember the first time you heard the life-changing words of John 3:16? Sometimes I wish I had been a fly on the wall, listening in and observing this mile-marking scene being played out in my own life. *Imagine.* The hope of glory spelled out in one unassuming string of letters and spaces. Honestly, I'm not sure I can pinpoint the first moment someone shared this passage with me, although I can promise you it was before I could either read or write. Somewhere between Pampers and pre-school, the fact that God loved us so much that He provided Jesus as our path to salvation was embedded into the deepest, most foundational truths of my life. I trust in that certainty today. There's really no mystery as to why this simple string of words from the middle of John chapter 3 holds the top place among the verses much of the world knows by heart. After all, this particular sentence reveals the reality of God's plan of redemption, and the essence of the Christian faith message.

My own heritage of faith has spurred me on to sharing the hope of salvation with the next generation; sharing my beliefs with the child I've been privileged to birth and nurture. The coolest thing about being a mom is the honor of passing on the truths that have impacted my life. Near the back of the lower drawer of my jewelry box, next to a pair of earrings and a cute silver bracelet, a precious treasure is stored. A simple wooden heart with a few layers of craft paint and a stick-on clasp backing proclaims the hope of salvation. The pin our son and I assembled years ago while attending our church's Easter celebration holds a priceless place in my heart. This bright red shape with a simple handwritten "John 3:16" is a mother's reminder of the first time she shared this life-giving verse of salvation's promise with her son. As he sat on my lap in that church fellowship hall, watching me write a life verse on the heart cutout he had so carefully painted, my emotions were dancing as the joy of inspiring a new generation began.

Does Owen remember that day? I assure you, he doesn't.

But I do.

God does.

Jesus still smiles about it.

The words of hope spoken forth and planted in the fertile soil of a growing mind have taken root and impacted the rest of his days. As I watch our son grow into a mighty man of God, I praise the Lord for the early days of foundation building and seed planting. Now that the branches of his life experiences are reaching out into the world around him, I have confidence in knowing that Owen knows who his Maker is, and that his Creator loves him more than the world could ever fathom.

Such words of affirmation concerning a God who loves us beyond our wildest dreams are worth hearing over and over with fresh ears. The truth of God's love has the ability to revive the weariest heart.

DAY ONE

SEEKING THE SAVIOR - JOHN 3:1–21

The Focus Verses:

For God so loved the world, that He gave His only begotten Son, that whoever believes in Him should not perish, but have eternal life. **John 3:16**

Jesus answered and said to him, "Truly, truly I say to you, unless one is born again, he cannot see the kingdom of God." John 3:3

The Main Thought:

God answers our questions.

The Story within the Story:

I believe one of the most difficult aspects of growing in our Christian faith is the danger of becoming complacent about the truth we already know. How easy would it be to read John 3, and skip the 16th verse, simply because we've known it by heart our whole lives? Thinking that we already know about Jesus because we've learned a list of Bible verses and lived through a few seasons of vacation Bible school is a trap that the devil loves to set. If the enemy can get us to take our eyes off the miraculous truth of the gospel message and demote the promise to a mere statement instead of a praise-filled proclamation, then he's decidedly winning the fight for our attention.

Even as you read this page, I venture to guess that there is an element of your mind that is bored of reading about John 3:16, yet again. Why? Has the promise of God's redemptive plan for mankind lessened any since Jesus proclaimed the hope of salvation to Nicodemus? Did the mighty Pharisee, Nicodemus, not find this truth worth the risk of hiding in the shadows of the moonlit night? He did. So, two thousand years later, why do we not find it worth our *full* attention?

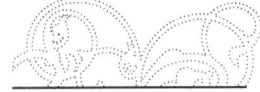

What is the most familiar to us can easily become the most easily overlooked.

I say such a bold statement only because, if I'm not careful, I find myself grabbing the oar handles and rowing my own boat of apathy. The most familiar to us can easily become the most easily overlooked. Yet, as we learn more about God, His Son, and His Word, everything about the Scriptures points us back to John's gospel, and the hope found in the third chapter. God has given us His Word to point us to Jesus. God gave us Jesus to point us to salvation. God gave us salvation so we could enter a restored relationship with Him and enjoy eternity in heaven with the Father, Son, and Holy Spirit. So, my friend, this familiar verse, the very one we know by heart over every other verse, is our lifeline to the Father. It is our hope, our promise of grace, and our picture of mercy. It's all about Jesus.

In my first Bible study, *Life Principles for Christ-like Living* I take the reader through an in-depth look at all the 3:16 verses of the New Testament. While this adventure is a comprehensive and exciting one, one of my favorite chapters in that work is, unsurprisingly, the focus on John 3:16. Why? God's love for us jumps off the pages of Scripture in the verses of John chapter 3, and our hope is written in ink that can never

VERSES WE KNOW BY HEART

fade. In our journey together, we will take a bit of a different approach, but with an equally investigative eye for the life application principles found in God's promise to us.

Take a moment to read John 3:16, phrase by phrase. How would you separate out the four sections of this verse?

1. _____

2. _____

3. _____

4. _____

We will spend our week going through these different segments of our well-known sound byte, John 3:16, digging for morsels of the miraculous within the verse we know so well. As we look at little clips of our verse, we'll also check out the background information concerning the context, purpose, and intent of the verse's content as it is confirmed in John 3:1–21.

But first, let's discover why we need to be born again. Today, we' take a specific look into the concept of being born again, and we'll look into the curiosity of a man that spurred this conversation with Jesus. We'll understand the whole passage in context, so that we'll be better equipped to tackle the sections one at a time for the rest of our week together.

WEEK ONE

The Passage:

Read John 3:1–21. Write down key points from the text and journal your thoughts about what you have read:

_____

_____

_____

_____

The Details:

1. What question/statement does Nicodemus ask in John 3:2? What was Jesus' response, and how did Jesus use this question and answer to open up dialogue about the concept of salvation?

_____

_____

_____

Did Jesus seem upset about answering the questions of a religious leader?

_____

_____

_____

How does this story about Nicodemus provide us with a clearer understanding of salvation?

_____

_____

_____

VERSES WE KNOW BY HEART

2. What specific questions have you or your acquaintances had about the idea of eternal salvation? How did those questions get answered (and who provided insight)?

_____

_____

_____

How does John 3:1-21 in particular answer questions about the possibility of eternal life?

_____

_____

_____

3. The term "born again" is a stumbling block to some unbelievers who can't grasp what the words imply. How does Jesus explain the process of being "born again" to Nicodemus?

_____

_____

_____

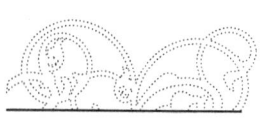

Merriam–Webster's Collegiate Dictionary defines atonement as "the reconciliation of God and mankind through the sacrificial death of Jesus Christ."

A Closer Look:

When Jesus describes the process of being brought into relationship with God through salvation, He uses the peculiar phrase, "born again." *Born again* has nothing to do with our initial physical birth and everything to do with a brand new start on life spiritually. As we are "born" into the family of God through our acceptance of the sacrificial atonement found through Jesus Christ, we spiritually shift our family heritage from the family of earth to the family of God. Our lives that were once filled with the darkness of this world are flooded with the light of life. The Holy Spirit dwells within us at the moment of conversion until the moment we leave this earth. We are new creations in Christ Jesus!

The Bible Knowledge Commentary shares the following: "to be **born again** or born "from above" (***anōthen*** has both meanings; i.e., "from above"… and "again"…) is to have a spiritual transformation that takes a person out of the kingdom of darkness and into **the kingdom of God** (cf. Col 1:13)."

WEEK ONE

A Question for Your Life Today:

Read 2 Corinthians 5:17. In relation to our standing as "born again" believers, how does this verse comfort you as a Christian? Where are the sins of your past?

_____

_____

DAY TWO

THE INCREDIBLE LOVE OF GOD - JOHN 3:1–15

The Focus Verses:

For God so loved the world… John 3:16

…that whoever believes may in Him have eternal life. John 3:15

The Main Thought:

God loves the world, and everyone He has created.

The Story within the Story:

Do you wonder if God really loves the world? The easiest way to observe the reality of this love is to gaze upon the morning's sunrise over the ocean, or the multicolored display of a magnificent sunset. Or passing by the fragrance of a summer bloom as it stretches upward to the heavens. Or pondering the complexity of the human body, and how the Lord fashioned us into existence with the dust from the earth, breathing life into Adam and giving him a helpmate named Eve.

God didn't have to create the world, and everything in it. *He just did.* In the blink of an eye, the God of all Creation decided, for His own pleasure, to create the sun, moon, stars, earth, and all we know to be. Why? Because He felt like it. Out of His great love for us, God made us.

What is your reaction to the phrase, "because He felt like it?" Is that kind of motive hard to believe? Our Almighty Father's ways are not our ways. His thoughts are not our thoughts. We will only know why God has placed the earth in orbit when we get to heaven—until then, we'd be better off simply acknowledging that God has done what He has decided to do. Just like parents, locking eyes with children who press for answers, God says, "Because I said so." His heart is set on forging a relationship with His creation; with you and me. And He has provided the means to do so through the perfect sacrifice of Jesus Christ, His Son.

In today's passage we'll read with fresh eyes and tender hearts about the exchange between Nicodemus and Jesus. The stage is set and the scene unfolds. In the silent protection of nightfall, a man asks his Savior a few questions. *How can it happen? How can this be?* And, with all the love a perfect Son of God can give, Jesus answers, "Because the Father said so."

The Passage:

Reread John 3:1–15. What new information do you see about the exchange between Jesus and Nicodemus? Write down new points from the text and journal your thoughts about what you have read:

_____

_____

_____

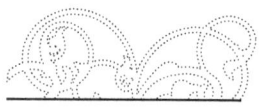

Out of His great love for us, God made us.

The Details:

1. What was Nicodemus's spiritual background and religious title? (See John 3:1)

_____

_____

_____

WEEK ONE

2. Why do you think he talked to Jesus under cover of darkness?

___

Would the fellow Pharisees have been pleased with Nicodemus asking about the teachings of Jesus? Why or why not?

___

3. Let's think about the apostle Paul for a minute. Read Paul's description of his own religious credentials in Philippians 3:4–7. What was Paul's religious background, and what was his reaction to his own earthly accomplishments compared to the truth of the gospel, for the "sake of Christ"?

___

4. Now think about Nicodemus's resolve to search for the truth, despite his success as a Pharisee. Have you had times when you've called out to God in the quiet hours of the night, even when your life seemed to be great on the surface? Describe one of those times and how the Lord answered you:

___

VERSES WE KNOW BY HEART

A Closer Look:

It is really easy to trust in our titles, accomplishments, and achievements. The world exalts the things of man, and the initials after our names serve to point out the expertise we've gained in the wisdom and knowledge of the world. In God's economy, though, all those titles, certificates, degrees, and accomplishments can become a slippery slope of pride if we get our heart's focus mixed up.

I brought in the verses from Philippians to show the other side of spiritual excellence. Paul gives us a picture of an ego in check—of a man who understands that the highest honor we can ever be bestowed this side of heaven is the title of *believer*, of *Christian*. All the earthly titles and family lines in the world are great, but they can't bring salvation. Only Jesus has provided a path to eternity in heaven. Though old Nic's Pharisaical buddies were intent on showing Jesus they were religiously superior to Him, Nic humbled himself like Paul, and set his titles aside for a moment of moonlit transparency. And I think we're in great company when we do the same. Let's set aside our quest for the nods and winks of man's approval, and set out to discover what pleases the heart of God. Let's live life for the sake of Christ.

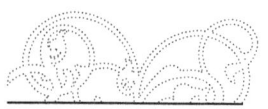

Let's live life for the sake of Christ.

A Question for Your Life Today:

What answers do you need from God this week? Write out a prayer to the Lord, asking Him to provide clarity, direction, and answers:

_____
_____
_____

DAY THREE

JESUS THE SON OF GOD - JOHN 3:16–17

WEEK ONE

The Focus Verses:

...that He gave His only begotten Son... John 3:16

For God did not send the Son into the world to judge the world, but that the world should be saved through Him. John 3:17

The Main Thought:

God gave His only Son for you!

The Story within the Story:

In a childhood movie, *Willy Wonka & the Chocolate Factory,*[a] a golden ticket is sought to pay entrance to a magical land filled with candy and wonder. After ripping open the outer wrapper and watching the metallic paper glisten in the sun, a young boy named Charlie almost misses his destiny when the ticket escapes his grasp. Voucher in hand once again, the child with the prize celebrates with family about his new found position in life. Though he is one of the least likely winners in the world, the boy is brought forward and given honor. Lumped together with other winners from various backgrounds of affluence and spoilage, the humble Charlie is the one character who moves through the experience with integrity and humility. In the end, he is found to be truly the most deserving of them all. But what if he hadn't discovered the magic ticket? What if Charlie never made it to the chocolate factory?

What if we, as a people who are desperately hoping to find the secret ticket to salvation, never purchased the right candy bar? What if it was all left to probability? Friends, many faith traditions in our world throughout the ages have set up exactly this kind of system. They have bought into the storyline that only by a hopeful possibility will they escape death, or inferior reincarnation, or punishment. This unhealthy game of chance, otherwise known as earned salvation through good works, does have the lure of gaining the adherents access to golden tickets. But, though these tickets supposedly get them to the opulent palace gate, they are still less than secure about their eternal outcome. Why? Those golden tickets never atone for sin, nor do they provide the only path to salvation and a relationship with the One True God.

Today we will discover the two verses that provide hope to the hopeless, atonement for the sinful, and salvation for the human race. All these promises await those who believe in the gift of salvation given through the shed blood of Jesus Christ, God's Son.

I'm not talking about a system of chance, luck, contests and winners, or golden tickets. We will discover a trust in truth, power, and grace; a gift of mercy extended by a loving and all-powerful God.

The Passage:

Reread John 3:16–17. What other details about salvation do you notice this time? Why was Jesus sent? Write down key points from the text and journal your thoughts about what you have read:

_____

_____

_____

_____

The Details:

1. Why did God send Jesus, according to John 3:16–17?

_____

_____

2. Did Jesus come to condemn or save?

_____

3. What is Jesus saving us from?

_____

4. What benefits do we receive from salvation, according to verse 16?

_____

5. What do you think eternal life with God will be like?

A Closer Look:

We could easily spend an entire six-week study examining the wonder and miracle of salvation. We could go through the countless evangelistic systems and formulas for explaining how to receive Christ Jesus as our Savior. For simplicity's sake, we won't compare the popular evangelistic outlines, or even list them all here. Let's look at a combination of the basic steps we need to take in order to accept Jesus Christ, enter into a relationship with Him, and follow Him:

- Admit that all are sinners and fall short of the glory of God (Romans 3:23).

- Understand that God has provided the gift of salvation for all who have sinned, and those who do not accept this gift will experience death (Romans 6:23).

- Accept the fact that Jesus paid the price for our sin, and came to save us from that sin, and leads us to eternal salvation (John 3:16–17).

- Understand that Jesus died once for all sin (Romans 6:10).

- Understand that we are saved by grace through faith, not by works (Ephesians 2:8–9; Romans 5:1).

- Understand that Jesus is the only path to salvation (John 14:6).

- Repent of our sins, and confess with our mouth that Jesus is Lord (Romans 10:9; Mark 1:15).

- Allow Jesus to be Lord of our lives, and commit to obediently following His precepts (Ephesians 2:10; Matthew 28:19–20).

What are the main points we take from this summary?

- We are lost without a Savior.
- We need a Savior. Jesus is that Savior.
- Our Savior has provided a way of atonement; a path to everlasting life.
- We come to Jesus through faith, not works, and no other belief system leads to the Father.
- We have a choice accept or reject the gift that is given.

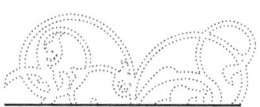

If you haven't made the decision to follow Christ, what issues are holding you back from saying yes to salvation?

Which will you choose? Which have you chosen? I pray right now, before we go any further together, that you have made this eternity-affecting decision to follow Christ; to accept the gift of salvation. I pray that you have gone beyond simply knowing this verse by heart to having the truth within this verse living inside you. God so loves *you* that He gave Jesus to die in your place, for your sin, on your behalf. He wants to spend eternity with you. No matter what you've done in the past, or what sins lay deep within the secret places of your past, *He can forgive.* God sent Jesus to save you. Jesus has paid the price, and His Father has forgiven you, if you've laid those sins at the foot of the cross. He desires to see you enjoy an eternal relationship with Him!

A Question for Your Life Today:

How has your life changed spiritually, emotionally, and physically since you accepted Jesus as your personal Savior? (Or, if you haven't made the decision to follow Christ, what issues are holding you back from that decision?)

_____

_____

_____

_____

DAY FOUR

FAITH'S TRANSFORMATION - JOHN 3:18

The Focus Verses:

...that whoever believes in Him shall not perish... John 3:16

He who believes in Him is not judged; he who does not believe has been judged already, because he has not believed in the name of the only begotten Son of God.
John 3:18

The Main Thought:

If you believe in Jesus, you don't have to fear death.

The Story within the Story:

It was one of those moments that I wouldn't trade for the world, and wouldn't ever want to repeat. I was with a mission team in the middle of the desert lands of Africa, and we were prayer walking through a medical compound. We noticed upon arrival that there were many men who wore matching head scarves with distinctive patterns we'd yet to see in this remote area, yet saw often on the evening news. The crowds of people were sitting around outside the buildings, either waiting for an appointment, or for family members.

Walking and silently praying from building to building, one thing stuck out in my mind. The men we first noticed were slowly disappearing from the crowds! They quickly and quietly left the area. The speckled view of colorful head coverings was dwindling, and now, only women and children were hanging out on the sidewalks and benches. We wondered where the men had gone, but tried to remain focused on our purpose for visiting the location.

VERSES WE KNOW BY HEART

As we were finishing up and walking through the last area, I noticed that one man wearing the distinctive scarf had returned, and was sitting outside the door of the building we were about to enter. While ordinarily this wouldn't cause alarm, on this occasion, my heart leapt inside me. See, along with the mysterious men, the other cars around our truck drove away while we were visiting the area. The sand lot around our car was empty except for our vehicle and a single white van that had parked beside my passenger door. The van was beat up with the windows broken out. It looked more like a bad scene from a movie than reality. I remember becoming filled with trepidation, and a cold sweat appeared on the brow of my warmed skin. The rest of our group was clearly less worried than I was. Maybe it was nothing, but only time would tell.

I looked at the team leader, and walked to our truck. What else could we do but calmly proceed with our day, as if we were unmoved? Walking in silence, I was less than silent inside. I was having a serious heart-to-heart with my Father in heaven. In the blink of an eye, God brought me to a very real moment of faith. I had but seconds to lay my fear at the feet of my Savior, and accept His strength in my time of weakness. Inside my mind I thought, for the first time in my life, "Lord, *if this is it*, I'm OK with that." It is impossible to fully convey how difficult that was to admit, or how freeing it was to embrace. I finally got what it meant to put your trust—even unto death—in God. How could I be so confident? My life doesn't end when I leave this earth. I have a hope of eternity, found only in Jesus Christ.

You know what? We were fine. The van sat there in the sand covered parking area as our truck rolled away. Nothing happened. I still don't know what the deal was with the men who were hanging around when we showed up and why they were in a rush to leave. It doesn't matter. All that matters, in my mind, is that God used the situation to grow my faith beyond anything I'd ever experienced. And He proved that, as we trust in Him, we have nothing to fear—not even death.

The Passage:

Reread John 3:18. What is the distinction between believer and non-believer? Write down key points from the text and journal your thoughts about what you have read:

_____

_____

_____

_____

The Details:

1. What do the words *condemnation* and *judgment* mean to you? What images or stories come to mind?

_____
_____
_____

2. Describe a time when you felt like a person was unjustly judging you in a situation and how you responded:

_____
_____
_____

3. In light of John 3:18, where did that condemnation and judgment come from? Jesus or Satan?

_____

4. How can you release or rise above unjust feelings of judgment? Who can help you gain freedom from such false accusations?

_____
_____

5. Read Romans 8:1. As we look into the concept of judgment and condemnation, how does this verse encourage you?

_____
_____
_____

VERSES WE KNOW BY HEART

A Closer Look:

The Bible Knowledge Commentary explains today's verse in the following way:

> The instrumental means of salvation is believing in the finished work of Jesus on the cross. But people who reject the light of the *Logos* are in the dark (John 1:5; 8:12) and are therefore **already** under God's judgment. They stand **condemned.** They are like those sinful, dying Israelites who willfully rejected the divine remedy (Numbers 21:4–9). A believer in Christ, on the other hand, is under "no condemnation" (Romans 8:1); he "will not be condemned" (John 5:24).

Jesus frees us from all condemnation and judgment. By believing in the name of Jesus Christ, the Son of God, we escape the looming cloud of judgment and enter into the light of God's grace. Praise God for His grace in your life today!

A Question for Your Life Today:

List some sins from your past that have caused you to feel condemnation, and then describe how God's grace and forgiveness in your life has cleared those looming clouds of judgment:

_____

_____

DAY FIVE

THE HOPE OF HEAVEN - JOHN 3:19–21

The Focus Verse:

…but have eternal life. John 3:16

But he who practices the truth comes to the light, that his deeds may be manifested as having been wrought in God. John 3:21

WEEK ONE

The Main Thought:

Jesus has given us access to salvation and the promise of everlasting life in heaven.

The Story within the Story:

The house was entirely too quiet. I should have known that something was terribly wrong by the silence wafting through the air. But as a young mother, I was thoroughly enjoying the break from chaos, calamity, and Cheerios. After a few minutes of sheer bliss, I wandered into the family room to assess the situation. In my mind, I figured I'd find three things: a toddler, a television, and (I was convinced), a looming tantrum. I was right.

The television was on, volume low, mumbling in animated tones to little ones who liked furry monsters and the alphabet. The boy, trying to hide the mess he'd made in silence, scooted to the left about a foot, sat on the box of chocolates he'd gotten into, and hid his hands from mommy's view. Slowly, his head raised inch-by-inch to reveal the proof of guilt. A beautiful smeary brown collage of goo was plastered to his face. He couldn't hide his grin (trouble never was his best-kept secret) and when his lips parted, he revealed cocoa-covered teeth and a tongue slathered in proof. Merely a second went by before the big tears came and the remorseful expression of guilt emerged. The funniest thing happened a moment later, when I asked him what he had done.

"Honey, did you eat all that chocolate without asking?" To me, this was a no-brainer. He was caught, brown-handed.

"No, momma. I didn't eat it all." He replied, mouth quickly turning from a chocolate deposit box to an overgrown frown.

"Now, Owen, I want the truth. Did you do it?" Nothing like a second chance.

"Ok, I did it, but I didn't eat it all. Look!" And with that, he lifted his behind off of the candy box to reveal the rest of the goods: a few in the box, and one or two stuck to the seat of his overalls.

Had I not asked, the guilty one would have hidden the proof, in an attempt to keep his sin silent. How often do we hide our own bad choices, only to find ourselves covered in proof and smooshing the leftovers of the pleasure we were seeking in silence. God can take away the most smeared-on sin in our lives and transform us into new creations of beauty—if we let Him.

VERSES WE KNOW BY HEART

The Passage:

Reread John 3:19–21. How will the life of the new believer be changed? What will capture our focus? Describe the difference between believer and unbeliever. Write down key points from the text and journal your thoughts about what you have read:

_____

_____

_____

_____

The Details:

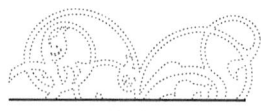

Walking in the truth of the gospel is revealed through our choices and actions.

1. Like our devotional story for today, sometimes we get caught hiding our sins. In John 3:19–21, what does God say about those who continue to hide sin? What is the root cause and motivation of their actions?

_____

_____

What does the passage reveal about those who live according to the truth?

_____

_____

2. In verse 20, why does the evildoer hide in darkness? What would happen if her deeds were exposed?

_____

_____

3. Look at verse 21. What do you think it means to have deeds that are "manifested as having been wrought in God" (NASB)?

_____

Walking in the truth of the gospel is revealed through our choices and actions. As obedient followers of God, our deeds will have an obvious connection to godly principles. We will live according to the precepts of Scripture, and our lives will show the fruit of a life lived with a biblical worldview. Therefore, our deeds will obviously be an outpouring of our relationship with Jesus Christ.

A Closer Look:

As we close this look at John 3, it is clear that there are two sides to this story of salvation. On one side of the spiritual coin of choices is the camp of those who refuse to leave the sin of this world. Judgment will come to those who stay in sin. Such refuters of truth will cling to the darkness that hides the sinful choices they make. They will flee the truth of the gospel, the body of believers, and will shun the thought of joining a congregation filled with Christ followers. The more sin invades a life, the more that life hides from the truth. After all, the truth condemns evil and exposes lies for what they are: sin.

On the flip side of the spiritual coin we have the believers who have trusted in Jesus, and entered into a personal relationship with Him. Instead of harboring shadows of sin lurking in plain view, these transformed creations follow Jesus in spirit and in truth. They have repented from past sins. There is no fear of walking in the light of life and in the fellowship of the gospel. Such believers experience the joy of fellowshipping with other likeminded Bible adherents. The truth is freedom to those who walk in it; there is nothing hidden in darkness that causes the person to shrink back. As we've learned this week, there is no condemnation for those who are in Christ Jesus (Romans 8:1).

The precepts of the Lord are not a stumbling block; they are an outline to a life full of freedom and integrity. They who walk in the light and are OK with the thought that their "deeds may be manifested as having been wrought in God" (John 3:21b).

The message of the gospel is:

Simple.

Profound.

Never boring.

Our relationship with God reveals the following:

- It is God's love that provided redemption through Jesus, His Son.
- It is our belief in the Son that keeps us from perishing.
- It is the Father's love for us, and the path through His Son, that gives us access to eternal life.

The message of the gospel is:

Simple.

Profound.

Never boring.

So, friend, why do we feel a temptation to yawn when reciting John 3:16? I haven't a clue.

A Question for Your Life Today:

Are you hiding any secret sins? Take a moment right now to confess those to the Lord, and ask Him to forgive you. He is faithful and able to forgive!

WORKS CITED:

Walvoord, John F.; Zuck, Roy B.; Dallas Theological Seminary: *The Bible Knowledge Commentary: An Exposition of the Scriptures*. Wheaton, IL: Victor Books, 1983–c1985, S. 2:281.

Willy Wonka & the Chocolate Factory. Directed by Mel Stuart. Written by Roald Dahl. Filmed by David L. Wolper Productions. Released 30 June 1971, USA.

Merriam–Webster, Inc.: *Merriam–Webster's Collegiate Dictionary*. Eleventh ed. Springfield, Mass.: Merriam–Webster, Inc., 2003.

Walvoord, John F.; Zuck, Roy B.; Dallas Theological Seminary: *The Bible Knowledge Commentary: An Exposition of the Scriptures*. Wheaton, IL: Victor Books, 1983–c1985, S. 2:282.

WEEK TWO

Connected to the Savior

Victory in Jesus

Romans 8:26–39

Children go missing. Tragedies strike. Sickness invades our families. The weather wreaks havoc on landscapes and communities. Crimes plague a nation, and compromise seems to win a little more of our minds with each passing day. What do we do? Throw up our hands in complete defeat, and go live in a cave somewhere? Sorry, wrong answer. *We press on. We search for hope.* Jesus is our perfect solution—our only source of true hope. (Contrary to popular film lines that assert than an old Jedi master would be the only hope.)

Life is hard. Even for Christians! Beyond tragedies, major unexpected events, and traumatic scenes that touch our lives like a hit-and-run gone bad, we have to endure daily struggles that wear on our strength and peace of mind. We don't enter into relationship with Jesus Christ and magically snap our fingers, instantly banishing the troubles of the world into obscurity. Sometimes drama seems to engulf the days of our lives more intensely than in the bizarre plots that drive daytime soap operas.

Sure, it's easy to be cheerful, positive, and focused on the victories in life when things are going great, but what about *those days*? You know, the days where everything goes wrong, your car won't start, and your hair won't look good, no matter how much goop you use? Even in our worst day and our ugliest hour, God is there for us, and we have victory in Him through Christ Jesus.

Truly, we do.

Victory is ours through Jesus Christ.

We win in the end.

This week I want all of us to think about a very important question: *Do we live each day in victory?* Take some time each day to ponder this question, evaluate your life and heart attitude, and really study the passage we have before us. I promise that believing this passage of Scripture will be life-changing. No more wondering if God is there. No more assuming that He isn't with you just because things are tough. You will be a lot more victorious living in the knowledge that no matter what, you belong to the King of kings, and are precious in His sight . . . even when your hair won't cooperate.

DAY ONE

I AM WEAK, BUT HE IS STRONG - ROMANS 8:26–28

The Focus Verse:

And we know that God causes all things to work together for good to those who love God, to those who are called according to His purpose. **Romans 8:28**

The Main Thought:

God uses every situation to show believers His love.

The Story within the Story:

On a bright summer day, rays of sunshine flowed over a brand new sundress with ruffles at the hem. A young girl skipped around in a pair of white patent Mary Jane shoes, white frilly socks spilling out of the tops. As her long flowing hair trickled through the air, the child ignored the rest of the world as she danced through the grass, spinning around with arms open wide, singing and smiling. Nursery rhymes, school songs, and church favorites; whatever melodies came to mind flew out her lips with a sweet sounding flair. A little girl's perfect day . . . *I remember it well.* And, as I danced in my favorite dress, I clearly recall singing "Jesus Loves Me" over and over while smiling up to the sky—knowing *He* was up there somewhere. On this day of pure joy, the words were a positive reminder of a love that was true.

As an adult, these same simple words find richer depth and meaning, as I mull the song over once more, with the commentary of an adult mind processing the truths in each verse:

Jesus loves me. *Even when I don't act like a good Christian?* Yes, always.

This I know. *Do I know? Or do I still question and doubt?* Lord, help me to continue to grow, and forgive me for my moments of unbelief!

For the Bible tells me so. *Oh, how I love God's Word.* Thank You God for revealing Yourself through the Bible.

Little ones to Him belong. *Lord, thank You for claiming me as Your daughter.* As a child and a grown up . . . I thank You for sheltering me safely in your love.

They are weak. *Weakness invades humanity, even in our best game of hide and seek.* Lord, show Yourself powerful through my many weaknesses. I need You.

But He is strong. *We serve a mighty God.* His powers are not weakened by my frail attempts to solve my own problems. He is not swayed by the lures of the enemy. The power of God is without end, and fully able to bring victory.

Yes, Jesus loves me. *Thank you Lord.* May I never forget this unbreakable promise.

God is made perfect in our weaknesses. Remember the childhood song? Indeed, Jesus loves us. We know He loves us because the Bible says so. We know Jesus loves us and we belong in Him. And, in the splendor of the simplistic verses, we sing that when we are weak, He is strong.

When we are weak, Jesus is strong.

Ever felt weak? I imagine that in times of difficulty, trial and crisis, feelings of weakness abound in your life, just as they do in mine. Yet in this weakness, Jesus is our strength. We are never alone! Can you fully imagine this promise? Even as I encourage you on your walk with the Lord, I am still working on internalizing this truth in my own life.

VERSES WE KNOW BY HEART

God is never weak, yet His people seem to continually find themselves in less-than-victorious situations. And in those very moments, God is our strength. He can use every event and interaction in our lives to show who He is, how much He loves us, and the depth of His grace.

The Passage:

Read Romans 8:26–28. Write down key points from the text and journal your thoughts about what you have read:

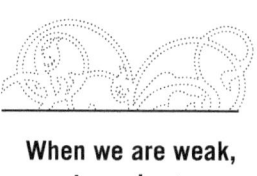

When we are weak, Jesus is strong.

_____

_____

_____

The Details:

1. To intercede means to act on another's behalf. In the context of Romans 8:26, when does the Holy Spirit intercede for us? How the intercession described?

_____

_____

2. Romans 8:27 refers to God as the one who "searches the hearts" and "knows what the mind of the Spirit is." The second part of that verse explains why the Spirit intercedes correctly, and is pleasing to the Father. Why is this? What does He intercede according to?

_____

_____

_____

The Holy Spirit needs to pray according to the will of the Father because He is joined with the Father as part of the Trinity. As God, the Holy Spirit is without error, and cannot lie. Describe the benefits and comfort of knowing that intercession on your behalf will be within the boundaries of God's will:

WEEK TWO

_____

_____

_____

3. We have heard verse 28 quoted many times in our culture. What does it mean to you, to hear that "God works all things together for good?" How does this comfort to you when you are struggling with a difficult issue or tough situation?

_____

_____

_____

At the end of Romans 8:28, we see that "all things work together for good to those who l_____ G_____, to those who are c_____ according to His purpose." How does this verse ending bring clarification the sound byte thought? _____

_____

_____

_____

_____

4. Do you live a life that reflects the understanding that God will use each of our situations for His good, revealing the purposes He has for our lives? Are you open in sharing with others in your sphere of influence the many ways God carries you through trials, and how He has blessed you in the midst of hardship? List ways that you share stories of God's goodness in your life with others:

_____

_____

27

A Closer Look:

The Apostle Paul understood weakness. The same minister of the gospel who challenges all of us with the truth we read today from the book of Romans also faced his own challenges. In fact, Paul states in 2 Corinthians 12:9 that after he pled with the Lord for help, the Lord spoke to his heart, saying, "My grace is sufficient for you, for power is perfected in weakness." As Paul traveled from town to town and region to region, sharing the gospel wherever he went, he encountered many hardships. Even in those tough moments in ministry, Paul still believed that he would "rather boast about [his] weaknesses, that the power of Christ may dwell in [him]" (2 Corinthians 12:9, brackets my addition).

When Jesus ascended to heaven, and sat at the right hand of the Father in victory over the grave, the Holy Spirit was sent to all believers. Since that moment, whoever believes and chooses to follow Jesus Christ the Son of God is given the Holy Spirit to guide and comfort them. In our passage today, we understand why this Spirit is needed. In our weakness, trials, and tough times, when we cannot even gather the strength to pray, God is with us—His Holy Spirit intercedes for us. We are not alone.

The Holy Spirit prays and intercedes according to the will of the Father. Jesus, during His earthly ministry, obeyed God completely, according to the will of the Father. Paul, even in his suffering and weakness, served the Lord and continually sought to live and minister according to the will of the Father. We too need to submit to the will of God, understanding that in every situation we face, God is with us.

A Question for Your Life Today:

How has God helped you become strong in a weakness? Describe the weakness and how God has equipped/helped/blessed you in that situation:

_____

_____

_____

_____

God is with us—His Holy Spirit intercedes for us. We are not alone.

DAY TWO

BECOMING MORE LIKE JESUS - ROMANS 8:29–31

The Focus Verse:

What then shall we say to these things? If God is for us, who is against us?
Romans 8:31

The Main Thought:

God is for the "whosoevers."

The Story within the Story:

Our All Powerful God had you and me on His mind before the world began. The plan of salvation through Jesus Christ was in place before Adam's garden grew. For all time, as the will of the Father unfolds, the sacrifice of Jesus Christ has been God's centerpiece of our world. Yet, we choose.

The Jews who walked the dusty roads along side the Messiah also had a choice:

- Accept.

- Reject.

- Listen and believe, or turn away and deny the truth.

As we discovered in Chapter 1, a leader named Nicodemus just had to hear the real story from Jesus's lips. Late at night, under the cover of darkness and the light of the gospel, the religious man found God . . . Jesus of Nazareth. Old Nic just *had* to ask the famous question of being born twice, and Jesus calmly explained the Christian's path to new life through the Son of God, and a new life through the water and the spirit. Whoever believes in him will not be separated from God—they will receive the gift of eternal life.

Whoever.

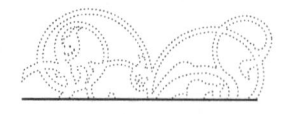

Everybody who repents and believes gets in. Quite a switch in thinking for Nicodemus, the exclusive Pharisee, don't you think? With the coming of the Messiah, salvation for all who would believe in Jesus became a reality—even for the Gentiles. The pearly gates were swung wide open for everyone who trusts Jesus as Savior. The Jews no longer had private access. Forgiveness could reach anyone, no matter how much of a heathen a person had been in their past, or how long their Gentile lineage flowed. Salvation now comes to the repentant, believing heart.

At the end of our life story, we have the promise of eternity in glory.

We are grafted into the family of God, adopted into His kingdom. As our passage for today reveals, we are called, justified, and will some day be glorified along with Jesus. Quite a promise, isn't it? At the end of our life story, we have the promise of eternity in glory. How sweet the promise of the grace of God; sweet and powerful the words of hope.

In light of this truth, we can look at these few verses for today's passage, and confidently shout with victory, "if God is for us, who can be against us?" In our darkest hour, the certainty of this proclamation will guide us to the Savior's comforting love.

The Passage:

Read Romans 8:29–31. Write down key points from the text and journal your thoughts about what you have read:

___

___

___

___

The Details:

1. Romans 8:29 mentions that those who believe will be "conformed into the image of His Son." What does that mean for us today, as we walk through each day, growing in faith?

_____

_____

What are some of the outward signs displayed when a person becomes more conformed to Jesus' image?

_____

_____

_____

As we grow in our knowledge of the Lord through his Word, through faith, and through the leading of the Holy Spirit, we will become more conformed to the image of Jesus. We will begin to pray more, follow God's will more steadily, cultivate a greater heart of compassion, and become more committed to sharing the gospel with the nations.

2. Verse 30 mentions that God "calls" us. In what specific ways has God called you to serve Him, and share the gospel?

_____

_____

_____

3. In what ways does God call all of us to share the gospel? Look up Matthew 28:19–20 for reference:

_____

_____

_____

VERSES WE KNOW BY HEART

4. God has *justified* us, or looks on us as innocent because of Jesus's sacrifice (verse 30). Think about that fact for a moment. How does it feel to know that your worst sin has been completely forgiven, and God looks at you as "innocent"? Journal any thoughts, and take time to praise God for His grace and your justification:

_____

_____

_____

_____

Because we are justified, we are seen as innocent in God's eyes. Romans 8:31 shows us that God's outlook is more important than any perception or accusation that can come from the world. The Father has final say, and He only sees a forgiven person, whose sins have been bought by the precious blood of His Son.

5. Describe a time when you thought the whole world was against you. Did verse 31 come to mind and bring you comfort? If not, how would this verse have helped you if you knew it at that time?

_____

_____

_____

_____

A Closer Look:

Today's passage has a lot of tough vocabulary and possibly a few new concepts for us. As we look through each verse, we find out how much God truly loves us, and has provided a way for us to have right relationship with Him. In the midst of all the grand theological discussions that could surround the concepts in this passage, the overlying truth is this:

God loves us.

He wants us to love Him.

If we accept and believe in Jesus, we share in His kingdom.

Through Jesus, God justifies us, and promises that we will be with Him in glory. And best of all, because of all this, we have victory in knowing that God is for us. With that truth, we also know that with Him on our side, it really doesn't matter who's against us, because we're on the winning team. We are children of God Most High!

A Question for Your Life Today:

Do you see yourself as the MVP (most valuable player) on God's winning team?

Yes _____ No _____

If not, pray that God will show you He is with you in the midst of your daily life.

DAY THREE

OUR HOPE IN CHRIST - ROMANS 8:32–34

The Focus Verse:

He who did not spare His own Son, but delivered Him up for us all, how will He not also with Him freely give us all things? **Romans 8:32**

The Main Thought:

God lavishes His love on us.

The Story within the Story:

Children aren't the only beneficiaries of a parent's generosity. The friends of the children also prosper by the decisions parents make. Owen and his best friend share many of the good things in life: movies, games, even summer road trips.

A few years ago we went on a road trip to Florida. We experienced theme parks, lots of amusement rides, swimming pools, fireworks displays, fun museums—the whole deal. Everywhere we went, our friend went. Everything we experienced, he experienced. And the gift shop moments? Sure, he got something equal to our son's gift choices. Why? Because the parents' generosity didn't stop with their own kid, but extended to the other child who was grafted into the family through relationship. While Owen benefits because he is related to us, the friend's connection to the beneficiary also reaps a harvest. Together, the boys enjoyed a fun vacation.

On the flip side of that relationship is a protectiveness that we have for this child, even though we are not his biological parents. We yearn to keep him safe when we are traveling. As parents, we love him like he's our own son, and have compassion when he's not feeling well, or having a bad week. We have cultivated a special place in our heart for this kid, and thank God that we've been able to watch him grow into a young man full of integrity and Christian values. Simply put, we're really proud of him!

While such a story pales in comparison to the gift God the Father has given us through relationship with His Son, we get a glimpse into the many things the Lord gives us that we just don't deserve. Because we are brought into the family of God through Jesus, we enjoy the benefits of being connected to God. His grace and mercy are unmerited and full of favor. Without the God of the Universe looking down with compassion on us all, we would have no hope in the world.

The Passage:

Read Romans 8:32–34. Write down key points from the text and journal your thoughts about what you have read:

_____
_____
_____
_____

The Details:

1. In Romans 8:32, what does it say God did to His Son? Why?

_____

WEEK TWO

2. What does the second part of Romans 8:32 tell us about God's love for us?

_____

_____

This verse points out that God will "freely give to us all things." What does that mean to you? Do you think this is limited to God's will for our lives, or is this a generic statement that guarantees our earthly desires will be met as well?

_____

_____

Who would dare mess with the people of God?

As we look at the truths of God's Word, we need to be mindful to understand these truths in context, and consistent with the whole of God's counsel. While God certainly wants us to be showered with His love and provision, segments of Scripture like this passage must not be taken in folly. God wants us to have a blessed life, but He will not "freely give us all things" that feed our earthly desires—God will provide and equip in the ways that will fulfill *His purpose* for our lives.

3. Verse 33 speaks of someone bringing accusations or charges against God's people. Think about a courtroom scene, with a plaintiff shouting damaging words at a defendant who is innocent. Now fill in the blanks for a similar scene. Imagine we are the defendants.

Who is the one who pleads our case (mediator? _____

Who is "the accuser of the brethren" (see Revelations 12:10)? _____

Who is the judge of all? _____

Romans 8:33 basically implies: *who would dare mess with the people of God?* The Lord's power extends beyond salvation, and into our daily needs. God has made us righteous through our relationship with Christ Jesus.

4. Romans 8:34 points out where Jesus is now. Where is He, and what is He doing there, on our behalf?

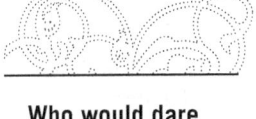

_____

_____

So as we think about that imaginary court case, if we are falsely accused by Satan, and Jesus intercedes on our behalf before the Lord, how will the scene play out? Who wins the battle? _____

Why? _____

_____

_____

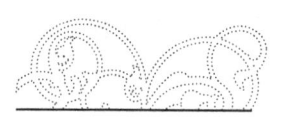

> "...let us also lay aside every encumbrance, and the sin which so easily entangles us, and let us run with endurance the race that is set before us, fixing our eyes on Jesus, the author and perfecter of faith, who for the joy set before Him endured the cross, despising the shame, and has sat down at the right hand of the throne of God" (Hebrews 12:1–2).

A Closer Look:

Our story for today gave us a simple comparison to the passage we studied, but I believe it brings forth a powerful thought. A friend gets good things because of his association to the one who is connected to the provision. God lavishes His love on us because of our connection to Jesus.

When the Lord looks at us, if we are in Christ, He sees us as not only believers, but Christians who are completely connected to Jesus Christ. Whatever the Lord has promised to Jesus, He has also promised to us. The hope of eternity is sealed in our connection to Christ.

God allowed Jesus to be sacrificed on our behalf, in order to bring us into right relationship with Him. When we recite John 3:16, we are repeating the promise that God has redeemed us through His Son Jesus, and Hebrews 12:1–2 remind us that through our precious bond we are able to come boldly before the Lord with any requests, needs, praises, and worship.

A Question for Your Life Today:

Read Hebrews 12:1–2. Picture Jesus seated at the right hand of the Father, interceding for you. Describe a past or present hurt, where you have been wronged by someone and need to allow Jesus to take charge of that situation, and free you of any residual hurt feelings:

_____

_____

_____

WEEK TWO

DAY FOUR

MORE THAN CONQUERORS - ROMANS 8:35–37

The Focus Verse:

But in all these things we overwhelmingly conquer through Him who loved us. **Romans 8:37**

The Main Thought:

Life isn't perfect, but God is!

The Story within the Story:

One morning in Bible study class, my friend Pat began to share from her heart about a trial her family had been through. As she began her story, I figured it would be another nice story about how God had provided for a family in need. I had no idea what she was about to reveal, or the magnitude of the strength her family had displayed in a time of great crisis.

See, a tornado blew through their town one Thanksgiving weekend years ago. By the grace of God, Pat and her family were visiting the grandparents, and were away from the scene when the whipping wind, rain, and clouds blew not just *over* her house, but *through* her house. By the time her husband drove down the neighborhood street, they realized life would never again be like it was before they packed their car for the holiday weekend. After showing identification, the police waved their car through the blockade, and the wheels slowly crept down the street. They were in shock. Houses were missing roofs and walls, and debris was scattered all over the place. Then, the car reached their driveway. *The house*. Where was the house? Pat's eyes scanned the scene. All that was left of the structure that used to be their home was the cement foundation. Pieces of their lives in the form of knick knacks, clothing, household goods, and memories were strewn across the yard, the neighborhood, and miles of countryside.

God provided for every need as this family rebuilt their lives. Not just a few meals; an abundance of meals. Every night they had a safe place to sleep. Every day as they collected the remnants of belongings, there were volunteers working alongside the family placing items into storage crates until they could sort through the stacks to find what was salvageable. The Lord preserved the family Bible, the wedding album, and a few other very tangible reminders that He was with them in the wake of this storm. Whatever they lacked, God was sure to provide in one creative way or another.

The most powerful testimony of this season of their lives was the Christmas card photo they chose to send out that year. See, nothing could steal the joy of the Lord from this family. They may never know exactly why the Lord allowed them to experience such loss and destruction, but in that moment they never doubted the Lord's presence and provision in their lives. And the photo showed this trust. Standing on the stark, empty foundation of what was once the family home stood two parents, two kids, and the golden retriever.

All smiling.

All joyful.

All praising the Lord.

I have to ask you: *in the same situation, would our expressions convey our joy in the midst of such loss?* In our human strength it would be impossible. But, as we live out these verses from Romans, I believe we would be equipped through the power of the Holy Spirit to endure. We would know what it is to "overwhelmingly conquer through Him who loved us" (Romans 8:37).

The Passage:

Read Romans 8:35–37. Write down key points from the text and journal your thoughts about what you have read:

_____

_____

_____

_____

WEEK TWO

The Details:

1. List the things we might think would separate us from Jesus' love as mentioned in Romans 8:35:

_____

_____

_____

2. Which of the things listed in your previous answer have you encountered recently? How did you react to this situation, and did you rely on Christ to deliver you?

_____

_____

The Complete Word Study Dictionary: New Testament defines the Greek term for "conquer," or huperniká, as "conquer, overcome. To more than conquer, utterly defeat (Romans 8:37)."

3. Most readers might have stories of distress or even peril, yet tribulation, famine, and sword are far-fetched notions in our comfort-driven lives. Take a moment to write out a prayer of thanks to the Lord for your safety and blessings:

_____

_____

_____

4. According to Romans 8:37, what outcome does Jesus provide?

We o_____ c_____ .

Does "overwhelmingly conquer" mean we'll have an easy life? _____

"We are more than conquerors..." (Romans 8:37 KJV).

A Closer Look:

Overwhelmingly conquering trials and tribulations through our relationship with Jesus Christ is not a guarantee that life will be rosy and void of any discomfort. The conquering power of Christ gives us the peace and assurance that no matter what we face this side of heaven, we have the guarantee of a glory awaiting us in eternity that cannot be shaken by the tough times of our earthly journey.

VERSES WE KNOW BY HEART

In Romans 8:36, Paul quotes Psalm 44:22, pointing out in the middle of this discussion about trials and triumphs, that it is for the sake of the Lord that we experience difficulties. Even still, no matter what we face, nothing can keep Jesus's love from carrying us to victory.

The Word says we will not only conquer, but utterly defeat! The love of Christ and His interceding power help us maneuver our way through life's hardships with the confidence and assurance that He is with us every step of the way. Do you need that encouragement today? I sure do! Together, we can rest assured that our situations are not unusual to God, nor are they too difficult for Him even within the most impossible scenarios fathomable.

A Question for Your Life Today:

When tragedy strikes, who do you turn to first: God or fellow man? Where should you look for answers and help? Why? _____

_____

_____

Commit to turn to God first in any situation that leaves you feeling defeated, persecuted, or bitter. Allow Him to equip you with conquering power to defeat the enemy's schemes!

DAY FIVE

SO HAPPY TOGETHER

The Focus Verse:

[Nothing] shall be able to separate us from the love of God, which is in Christ Jesus our Lord. **Romans 8:39 (brackets my addition)**

The Main Thought:

Nothing can separate us from the love of God!

The Story within the Story:

As a kid I remember well the miracle of making fruit punch concoctions. First, we took the plastic pitcher out of the cabinet. Then, we ripped open the little envelopes of colored dust, dumping the contents into the mixing vessel. I loved watching the mist of the powdery concentrate cascading through the air like a waterfall as it made its way to the container's bottom. Next, the scoops of sugar, weighing much more than the first ingredient, swished through the air and landed on top of the powder. Once that was done, we turned on the sink, and filled that container full of yummy, cool water. A quick whirlpool formed by a spinning wooden spoon, and voila! The drink was ready for preschooler consumption. The original ingredients were distinct when the process began, but after combining and adding water, a new drink was produced. If we wanted to get back to the separate pieces of our punch puzzle, we'd find it impossible to do so. The sugar was mixed. The concentrate was dissolved. The water had taken on the taste of the other two items.

Once we join in a relationship with Jesus Christ, we receive the Holy Spirit, and become a part of God's family. We are joined together with such a strong bond that nothing can separate us out again. We belong to the Lord. We've become a new creation. The Living Water (John 7:37–39) has transformed us into a wonderful follower of the Truth.

The Passage:

Read Romans 8:38–39. Write down key points from the text and journal your thoughts about what you have read:

_____

_____

_____

_____

VERSES WE KNOW BY HEART

The Details:

1. List all the types of things that can come against us, according to verses 38–39:

_____

_____

_____

2. The first four words of Romans 8:38 are: For I am c_____.

Are you convinced that none of the things mentioned can come between you and Christ?

_____

3. Our relationships with other people are separated by death, and our situations in life can be affected by other powers and created things, but nothing can separate us from the love of God. How does this encourage you when tough times occur?

_____

_____

_____

4. Describe a time when you felt like the world was coming against you, and how you rose above that negative onslaught of emotions:

_____

_____

_____

A Closer Look:

Ok, so I realize that an opening devotion about fruit punch mixing in a pitcher just doesn't cut it when we want to comprehend the magnitude of our abiding bond with

Christ. As we've looked at this passage from Romans this week, it is evident that Jesus not only "has our back" but is with us every step of our lives, in good times and bad. His love for us extends further than the good intentions of friends, and the obligation of earthly families. Jesus loves us enough to go to the cross for our sin, and enough to fight for our battles from here through eternity.

Again, I ask you: are you *convinced*? Completely steadfast in your faith and resolve that nothing, not even the cleverest schemes of the enemy, can come between you and Jesus Christ? Oh, that we would all have that confidence and boldness. Hopefully the lesson this week has carried each of us a little further on our journey to confidence in Christ.

John 10:10 tells us that Satan and any of his false teachers that try to steer us away from the truth of the gospel have come into our lives to "steal, and kill, and destroy" but that Jesus has forged a relationship with us "that [we] might have life, and might have it abundantly" (brackets my addition). With that gift of life in mind, Romans 8:38–39 lists a number of powers and authorities that could attempt to take our confidence, or steer us away from our victorious standing in the Lord. My question is simple: *do you believe that Jesus can handle your toughest trial?* Stand firm, my friend. Trust that His power is above all others. Call on His mighty Name.

A Question for Your Life Today:

Who can you encourage today? Who do you know that might be dealing with some sort of attack and that needs to hear about the conquering power available to those who trust in Jesus? In light of this week's lesson, what would you tell them about Jesus's presence in the midst of the trials of life?

_____

_____

_____

_____

_____

_____

WORKS CITED:

"Jesus Loves Me" by Anna B. Warner

Zodhiates, Spiros: *The Complete Word Study Dictionary: New Testament.* Electronic ed. Chattanooga, TN: AMG Publishers, 2000, c1992, c1993, S. G5245.

WEEK THREE

Blessed as a Believer

The Beatitudes

Matthew 5:1–12

The Sermon on the Mount: a familiar teaching of Jesus transcending time and culture, encouraging all who experience to find blessing in heartache, comfort in loss, and honor in humility. It is a message for the lost, hurting, and weary. It's an inspirational message for all believers. But is a sound-byte speech all these verses have for us? Does the surface story capture the full extent of the ink on paper that we read in our quiet time or the sermons we hear a pastor teach?

The Word of God is life. It is life-giving—inspiration breathed into our human existence in ways we cannot even comprehend. Just as soon as we think we have read all the Bible has to offer—every Scripture from cover to cover—and heard every sermon on Sunday, the Holy Spirit has a wonderful way of revealing yet another layer to the truths tucked away in God's Word as we faithfully read and study the Bible. A new breath of life bursts from the pages into our lives.

Not long ago I assumed that I had heard all there was to know about the Sermon on the Mount. Wrong! Sitting in a friend's Bible study class, listening intently to the teachings of "The Beatitudes" from the book of Matthew, this passage came alive like never before. My friend's teaching was incredible, but the chart on the chalkboard caught my attention the most. The different portions of the sermon were simply listed, but there was nothing simple about it. God captured my attention with the words on the wall. Staring at the list, it was clearer by the minute that I still had much to learn about this well-known passage. The hand-written chart on the board went something like this:

The Beatitudes: Blessings and Benefits

Blessed are those who (are) . . .	Because they will . . .
Poor in spirit	Have the kingdom of heaven
Mourn	Be comforted
Gentle/meek	Inherit the earth
Hunger and thirst for righteousness	Be satisfied
Merciful	Receive mercy
Pure in heart	See God
Peacemakers	Be called sons of God
Persecuted for faith	Have the kingdom of heaven

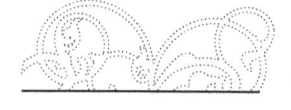

Sanctification: The term sanctification refers to the spiritual growth of a believer.

Somehow, seeing the connection between blessing and benefits made the whole theme of the Beatitudes solidify in my mind. Beyond the blessings was a pattern of growing in godliness as we mature in our faith.

Tucked inside these timeless teachings of the believer's attitudes to life are some of our most critical principles for godly living. The Beatitudes provide great insight and encouragement along with keys to understanding the Christian sanctification process. God is ultimately concerned with our spiritual growth; and Jesus, in His great wisdom and perfect standing in the will of God, is concerned with our sanctification as well. What better way to grow disciples than through a solid teaching of what the Christian life is like?

Warren Wiersbe explains the idea of godly living as shown in the verses for our week in the following way:

A. "Poor in spirit" (v. 3). Our attitude toward ourselves in which we feel our need and admit it.

B. "Mourn" (v. 4). Our attitude toward sin, a true sorrow for sin.

C. *"Meek" (v. 5)*. Our attitude toward others; we are teachable; we do not defend ourselves when we are wrong.

D. *"Hunger and thirst" (v. 6)*. Here our attitude toward God is expressed; we receive His righteousness by faith because we ask for it.

E. *"Merciful" (v. 7)*. We have a forgiving spirit and love others.

F. *"Pure in heart" (v. 8)*. We keep our lives clean; holiness is happiness to us, and we want no substitutes.

G. *"Peacemakers" (v. 9)*. Christians should bring peace, between people and God and between those who are at odds with each other. We share the Gospel of peace.

H. *"Persecuted" (v. 10)*. All who live godly lives will suffer persecution.[a]

Journey with me this week as we not only look to the familiar verses of a timeless mountainside sermon delivered by Jesus, but also dig deeper into the big picture of God where we discover a clever yet subtle teaching of the process of sanctification . . . hidden right before our eyes.

DAY ONE

BLESSED IN SEEKING GOD - MATTHEW 5:1–4

The Focus Verse:

Blessed are the poor in spirit, for theirs is the kingdom of heaven. **Matthew 5:3**

The Main Thought:

Seek God.

VERSES WE KNOW BY HEART

The Story within the Story:

We've all seen them. The three-year-old darlings who insist they can do everything themselves. *No mommy, I do it . . . I tie my shoes . . . no Daddy, don't help . . . I eat it with my fingers . . . no Mommy, I don't wanna have Sissy help me on the playground*; on and on it goes. More often than not, the little independent one finds himself changing his insistence on freedom when confidence outweighs skill. *Mommy, can you help me now? Daddy, I can't do it! Sissy, can you come here?*

Imagine the spiritual struggle that goes on in the mind throughout our younger years. We all begin life much like those little sweethearts who think they can do everything on their own. The average person's internal dialogue ponders many things over a lifetime. Someone who hasn't yet heard the gospel may think of spiritual things in generic terms of good versus bad. *I've been good. Haven't done much bad stuff, been pretty nice to others, and kinda think about God, but don't know much about this religious stuff.*

The unbeliever doesn't realize the magnitude of eternal life choices. Then one day, someone tells us that because of the Fall—Adam and Eve's disobedience—we all have become separated from God. There's only one path to right relationship: through the shed blood of Jesus. To receive Christ, we first have to realize that we come to him as broken people—broken by our own spiritual sin. We are all sinners in need of a Savior, and the answer to that condition is salvation through His perfect sacrifice. We have a choice.

To repent and believe, or not to repent and believe; that is the question.

For atheists, the thought of needing God remains in the naïve self-reliance category of the three-year-old not needing his mommy's help. *Nope. Don't need it, I can do it on my own, no thanks to you. I've got it. Don't need your silly God. I can handle life on my own.* But can they? Can anyone handle eternity without God? Unfortunately, those who die while still denying Jesus as the Son of God will find that the one thing they'll be handling is an eternal separation from God…they will find the answer they stood so strongly against was truly the answer that would give them eternal life.

Today we will discover that this spiritual poverty, the absence of right relationship with God, is an important subject for the Son of God. It is His foundational thought as He begins to preach to the multitudes. In His love for mankind, the poor in spirit top the list of those who will be blessed by God. We need to know we need Him!

WEEK THREE

The Passage:

Read Matthew 5:1–4. Write down key points from the text and journal your thoughts about what you have read:

_____
_____
_____

Before we jump into this passage in Matthew, verse by verse, let's take a look at another account of blessings given by Jesus found in Luke 6:20–26.

Read Luke 6:20–23, and write out the four principles he mentions in his passage:

a._____
_____
_____

b._____
_____
_____

c._____
_____
_____

d._____
_____
_____

VERSES WE KNOW BY HEART

Now read Luke 6:24–26 and list the four woes mentioned in this same passage:

a._____
_____
_____

b._____
_____
_____

c._____
_____
_____

d._____
_____
_____

What similarities do you see between the Beatitudes of Matthew 5 and Luke 6?
_____
_____
_____

What is different?
_____
_____
_____

WEEK THREE

The woes mentioned in Luke's passage are intended to admonish believers who are not living according to the precepts of the Lord. This is a message for those who are carnal Christians, looking out for their own selfish needs. Jesus is clear in both passages that blessings come to those who are genuinely following God. Luke reminds us that the Lord judges the intentions of our hearts and the purity of our motives, and isn't convinced merely by how spiritual we look to others. Unlike the Pharisees, who built their righteousness on adhering to laws and showing their spirituality, Jesus taught that godliness was cultivated from the inside out.

The Details:

1. Now go back to Matthew 5:1–2. Jesus settled down on the mountainside to teach. Though the multitudes were listening, who was Jesus's main audience and focus for the teaching?

_____

_____

Jesus directed His teaching to the twelve, to the broader audience listening on the mountainside, and also to us, we who read His Words today. We are His modern day disciples who are in need of instruction concerning godly living.

2. When you read the words "poor in spirit," what comes to mind? What kind of person do you picture? _____

_____

_____

_____

3. How does the implied sense of humility in the condition of poverty of spirit help one gain the kingdom of heaven? Describe the connection between being poor in spirit and humbling yourself in repentance of sin:

_____

_____

VERSES WE KNOW BY HEART

4. How does the previous question's answer relate to the discussion in Chapter 1 of God providing salvation for the "whosoevers"?

_____

_____

5. In Matthew 5:4 we switch to the next "beatitude" of mourning. Describe a time when you've mourned:

_____

_____

_____

6. How were you comforted during that experience? How did God provide special moments of comfort, or send extraordinary people into your life just at the right time, with the right words of encouragement?

_____

_____

_____

7. Think about mourning over sin. Have you mourned over the sins in your past? Write out some of the ways God has comforted you through the grace and mercy of His forgiveness:

_____

_____

_____

A Closer Look:

The first two principles listed in our week of blessings are the ideas of being poor in spirit and of mourning. As we relate these two ideas to our relationship with Jesus Christ, we see that our lack of godly connection does not leave us without an option; we have the choice to believe, and enter into the kingdom of heaven. Psalm 69:29–30, King James Version, tells us, "But I am poor and sorrowful; Let Your salvation, O God, set me up on high. I will praise the name of God with a song, and will magnify Him with thanksgiving." As we understand our need for a Savior, we allow God to lift us up through His Son Jesus Christ.

Through today's study we also understand that mourning over our sin allows us the opportunity to be comforted by the Lord. Just as Jesus taught us in John 3:17, God isn't focused on condemning us and leaving us without a solution. After all, He sent Jesus to save us. So, as we mourn over our sin, our hearts will become compelled with the desire to lay that sin down, and embrace the comfort given by God.

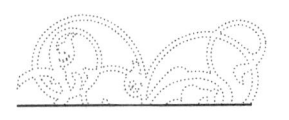

Jesus came to save the world, not to condemn it.

A Question for Your Life Today:

If you were sitting in a coffee shop, and a complete stranger seated at the next table told you she had a great job, and a nice life, but felt "empty inside," what would you say? Would you share a testimony of your life experience during a personal crossroads of faith? How could you help her see her poverty of spirit, and show her that the One who could fill that void is Jesus?

_____

_____

_____

_____

_____

_____

VERSES WE KNOW BY HEART

DAY TWO

BLESSED BY DOING THE RIGHT THING - MATTHEW 5:5–6

The Focus Verse:

Blessed are those who hunger and thirst for righteousness, for they shall be satisfied. Matthew 5:6

The Main Thought:

God satisfies our spirit.

The Story within the Story:

Satisfaction is clearly a finicky thing. If we listen to the candy bar commercials, we will hear that only certain chocolate candies can satisfy our hunger. If we listen to the words of old rock songs, we'll hear that some just can't get any satisfaction. If we buy into a particular fast food commercial's ploy, we'll agree that we want to go to the one place that lets us have our sandwich exactly the way we want it, bringing mealtime bliss. If we look at the clothing styles coming and going faster than drive-through traffic, we'll understand that no particular fashion statement will fulfill the continual craving for looking stylish. This year's hot new style quickly becomes next year's outlet sale item. The world will tell us many things about the contented life; and the loudest message it screams is that nothing on this earth will satisfy us completely. There's always something newer, better, faster, or cooler waiting for us (and our pocketbooks) just around the bend.

God, on the other hand, is all about satisfaction. He longs for us to tap into true contentment and a rewarding life filled with an understanding that regardless of our earthly situation, we serve a God who will "supply all your needs according to His riches in glory in Christ Jesus" (Philippians 4:19). This in no way guarantees we'll get the newest handbag displayed in the glass case at the department store; it means that our Lord will meet the needs in our lives that drive our ability to fulfill His purpose for our lives.

WEEK THREE

The Passage:

Read Matthew 5:5–6. Write down key points from the text and journal your thoughts about what you have read:

_____
_____
_____
_____
_____

Does meek = weak?

The Details:

1. When looking at the term "meek" I'm afraid that, all too often, we think of it as a weakness. One of my favorite explanations of meekness in the Lord also deals with humility. Look up John 3:30. What does John the Baptist say about his relationship with Jesus? Who is more important, John or Jesus? How does this relate to our sense of meekness and gentleness?

_____
_____
_____

Meek people give God's will priority over their own will.

John's humbleness in acknowledging that Jesus was the focus of ministry and attention brings us to a closer understanding of being meek. As we live in light of the fact that the Lord's ways are best, we make decisions according to His wisdom. We give God's will priority over our own will.

2. In the world's eyes, do the meek in society make good leaders? What leadership skills do world leadership models look for?

_____
_____
_____

3. Connected to our focus today on being gentle, or meek, is the idea of hungering for righteousness. Before we dive further into this idea, what does the phrase "hungering and thirsting for righteousness" mean? Describe:

_____

_____

_____

4. When we have a painful hunger and deep thirst, we are empty, and in need of filling. We need fuel to help us thrive and survive. Hungering or longing for righteousness implies that we are desperate for a real relationship with God. Describe a time where you felt spiritually empty and needed to be filled anew with God's sustaining power and truth:

_____

_____

_____

4. Our prayer life and ultimately our daily life will reflect that Jesus is a priority when we desire honesty and justice according to biblical precepts. How does your life exhibit your desire for God and godly principles? What do others see in you that reflects your yearning for godliness?

_____

_____

_____

A Closer Look:

Meek believers are gentle when approaching God, not shaking two fists toward heaven every time difficulties arise. A gentle spirit inheriting the earth speaks of our abiding relationship with the Lord; whatever He has, we have, through an inheritance found by being grafted into His family as His children. We conquer our spiritual enemies through our gentle trust in God, not through a tough military mindset bent on causing destruction to defeat the enemy.

As gentle spirits who hunger and thirst for righteousness, we are in constant pursuit of God's truth. We long to abide in His Word, live according to His will, and impact the world with His message of the gospel. We anticipate seeing others come to a saving knowledge of Jesus Christ. We are hopeful that people will be transformed by the gospel. We commit to living each day in light of eternity, and with a steadfast resolve to follow Jesus no matter the cost. And what are the benefits of living according to today's verses? We will walk as children of God with a satisfaction only the Lord can provide.

A Question for Your Life Today:

Do you feel satisfied with your life? If so, write a letter of praise to God. If not, write a letter to God asking Him to bring a sense of contentment and satisfaction to your soul today:

_____

_____

_____

DAY THREE

HEART FILLED WITH PRAISE - MATTHEW 5:7–8

The Focus Verse:

Blessed are the merciful, for they shall receive mercy. **Matthew 5:7**

The Main Thought:

God honors those who show mercy.

VERSES WE KNOW BY HEART

The Story within the Story:

God's mercy has been extended to us in great abundance, but what do we do with it? Do we turn to those who are in need and show them the same sense of compassion and help?

He has given us instruction on how to bless others as He has blessed us. Jesus enjoyed sharing spiritual truths through story. One such story, or parable, dealt with the issue of mercy and forgiveness (Matthew 18:21–35).

In the passage's context, Jesus is answering Peter's question about forgiveness, and spins a tale to make the answer poignant. A king was settling accounts. One of the servants simply couldn't pay the money owed (millions of dollars), and began begging for help. *Patience! Mercy! Just a little more time, please!* We can hear the childlike pleas that must have flowed from the desperate lips of the servant. The master let the servant go, giving him a settled account and a huge extension of grace and mercy.

The servant, in spite of this favor, ran out and found somebody who owed him a few dollars, and choked the poor debtor for the pittance he was due. The suffering debtor asked the servant for patience, in the same manner the servant had just asked of the master. Do you think the servant realized the error of his ways? Not a chance. He forgot what mercy looked like, and threw that poor debtor in prison until the payment could be scrounged up from somewhere.

You know, our actions always have a way of telling on us. That master who had been so nice to the servant in debt by the millions found out that his forgiveness wouldn't even be extended to another person for a few dollars. The master changed his mind, and instead of forgiving the debt, he threw the unmerciful servant in jail too, and made sure he was tortured until all the money owed was paid back.

What is the moral of the story? As Jesus told the parable, we learn that "this is how my heavenly Father will treat each of you unless you forgive your brother from your heart" (Matthew 18:35, New International Version). Today we'll learn about mercy, and having a pure heart. The benefits far outweigh the temptation to side with the world's ways of getting ahead. Let's choose mercy!

The Passage:

Read Matthew 5:7–8. Write down key points from the text and journal your thoughts about what you have read:

WEEK THREE

The Details:

1. Read Matthew 18:21–35. Today's story outlined this parable, but what additional things do you learn about mercy through this parable? What was the master's response to the one who had received mercy, but failed to extend mercy to his fellow man?

2. Because we have a relationship with Jesus, and the Holy Spirit dwells in us, we are able to extend compassion to others. What does Matthew 5:7 tell us will happen when we are merciful to others?

3. God has been compassionate to us, and we in turn are to be merciful to others. Look up 2 Corinthians 1:3–5. What does that verse tell you to do when God comforts you, or shows mercy to you? Are you only expected to receive from the Lord, or does the Word tell you to share that kindness with others?

"He who has clean hands and a pure heart . . . He will receive blessing from the LORD and vindication from God his Savior" (Psalm 24:4–5, NIV).

VERSES WE KNOW BY HEART

4. Compare the concepts of being merciful and being pure in heart. What similarities do you see between the two? What differences?

_____
_____
_____

5. What is the benefit of having a pure heart, as found in Matthew 5:8?

_____
_____
_____

6. Read Psalm 24:3–5. What does a believer with pure heart and clean hands experience?

_____
_____
_____

A Closer Look:

We are saved because a merciful God, full of grace, has extended a hand of forgiveness through the sacrificial blood of Jesus. It is only because God showed us mercy that we receive eternal life. Because of that extravagant grace and mercy, we should be compelled to extend mercy to our fellow man. As we like to say in so many other cases, "it's the least we could do." Really, friend, it's the least we could do!

Partnered with the mercy we gain and give is our resolve to live pure lives before the Lord. Daily repentance and an active prayer life give us a glimpse of God's direction for our lives. The more we determine to live with pure hearts, daily cleansed of sin and wrong motives, the closer we will be to understanding the will of God.

His purpose for our lives will become clearer.

His desires for our lives will be better understood.

His plan for our days will be obvious.

His message will ever be on our lips.

A Question for Your Life Today:

What does "seeing God" look like in your life? How does your commitment to God lead you closer to the Lord?

_____

_____

_____

DAY FOUR

AUTHENTIC PEACE - MATTHEW 5:9–10

The Focus Verse:

Blessed are those who have been persecuted for the sake of righteousness, for theirs is the kingdom of heaven. **Matthew 5:10**

The Main Thought:

God is the source of our strength.

VERSES WE KNOW BY HEART

The Story within the Story:

Christian author Randy Alcorn has a tremendously powerful fiction work titled *Safely Home*.[b] Though it is an imaginary story set in China, the truth of what the persecuted church endures jumps off the pages of the novel from beginning to end. Readers follow the storyline through hidden church meetings and scenes with imprisoned believers, and better understand the plight of brothers and sisters of our faith who face daily persecution because they have placed their trust in Jesus. The impact of the plot is heightened by the sense of peace of the main character, Li Quan, in the midst of persecution.

In one of the prison scenes tucked into *Safely Home*'s pages, Li Quan is brought before the warden to be disciplined after being forced to write a confession. When the warden reads the letter and finds it to be more of a profession of faith, he wants to inflict harsher punishment on the innocent prisoner. When confronted with proof of his rebellious actions, Quan replies with the following statement: *"You can kill me only if Yesu allows it, but you cannot kill his church. The early Christians said, 'The blood of the martyrs is the seed of the church.' When each martyr dies, a thousand Christians rise to stand in his place"* (p. 313). This work is a fictional story riddled with depths of truth. Truly, throughout the ages, when the persecuted church has paid the ultimate price for faith, God raises a new generation to proclaim the gospel. The power of God cannot be defeated.

Beyond this literary work, we have many avenues to discover what the persecuted church endures in our generation. Organizations such as Voice of the Martyrs[c] distribute information on the plight of victimized Christians around the world. Countless other missions and ministry organizations commit their time and energy to helping fellow believers around the world with literature, short-term team assistance, and long-term provisions.

What do all who are persecuted for the sake of Christ have in common? According to the Beatitudes of Matthew 5, those who suffer because of their faith are rewarded with the kingdom of heaven. This world is not their home. Eternity with the Lord is the prize they cling to, the hope that propels them on in their momentary struggles.

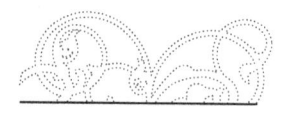

> **Being a peacemaker means we bring the peace of God to others.**

The Passage:

Read Matthew 5:9–10. Write down key points from the text and journal your thoughts about what you have read:

WEEK THREE

The Details:

1. Matthew 5:9 mentions peacemakers. *The Complete Word Study Dictionary: New Testament* describes this term in the following way: *"The one who, having received the peace of God in his own heart, brings peace to others (only in Matt[hew] 5:9). He is not simply one who makes peace between two parties, but one who spreads the good news of the peace of God which he has experienced."*[d] In light of this definition, is peacemaking more about pleasing others, or pleasing God? Why?

2. How has God brought peace to your life? How can you share this testimony with others?

3. Read Acts 16:16–24. In this scene, why are Paul and Silas being persecuted? What happens to them?

4. According to Acts 16:18–19, what was the real cause of the persecution?

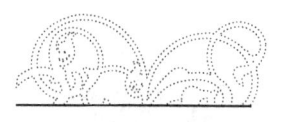

> "He ought to die because He made Himself out to be the Son of God" (John 19:7).

5. Reading further, in Acts 16:25–40, how did Paul and Silas become peacemakers while being persecuted for their faith?

_____

_____

_____

6. How does this passage from Acts reveal why unbelievers persecute Christians? Is it always because of the message of the cross, or also because of insecurity or other perceived threats to tradition and custom?

_____

_____

_____

7. Take a moment to think about the persecution Jesus suffered for His faith, and for our redemption. (Read John 18–20 for background.) What comfort do you receive in knowing that your sufferings and hardships are fully understood by Jesus, who humbly suffered more than anyone for our sake?

_____

_____

_____

Jesus now sits at the right hand of the Father in heaven. He has shown us that the persecuted will inherit the kingdom of God. We, as God's children, share in this inheritance, and no amount of maltreatment can keep us from that promise.

A Closer Look:

Today we've looked at two aspects of dealing with adversity. First, we looked at peacemaking as a means of leading others to Christ. Second, we discovered how we can be blessed in the midst of being persecuted for the sake of Christ. We know that the believer's goal is to glorify God in any situation, and be a light in a dark world, even if that world is terribly, terribly dark.

A Question for Your Life Today:

How could you become more active in supporting the persecuted church around the world? What will you commit to do today?

_____

_____

_____

DAY FIVE

INSULTS AS BLESSING? - MATTHEW 5:11–12

The Focus Verse:

Rejoice and be glad, for your reward in heaven is great, for so they persecuted the prophets who were before you. **Matthew 5:12**

The Main Thought:

God understands how you feel when you're persecuted for your faith.

The Story within the Story:

His roommates tried everything they could in an attempt to make his life difficult. They ate his food, leaving him hungry. They victimized him by teasing him relentlessly. His body was beaten, kicked, and hit whenever an opportunity to attack arose. His sheets were taken from bed as soon as he'd put everything in place each morning. Whatever the troublemakers could think up, they did—all because he was a Christian! The young believer was intent on following Christ no matter what words, insults, and hurtful actions came his way. His only Bible never left his sight—that was one thing he simply wouldn't allow the enemy to take from him. Night after night and day after day, the young man trusted the Lord to carry him through the discomfort and slander. He read the Word of God with dedication and zeal; he knew God would help him survive the constant badgering of mean-spirited roommates.

Then, one day, the chief persecutor of the band of boys wanted to know why this young Christian never retaliated. Why would he take all this undue punishment? The harasser became the student. He asked many questions under the protection of secret meetings. For the next few months the victim taught the bully about Jesus. You know what? A miraculous thing happened. The bully became a believer. He turned from the false faith of his fathers, and trusted in Messiah Jesus. All because one boy, who was persecuted for his faith, stood firm; just like many before him. And, in an ultimate act of faith, forgiveness, and mercy, the young witness gave his prized possession, his Bible, to the boy who tried so hard to destroy his faith. That new believer trusted in the Word that was given him, and is now fighting his own battle of faith in a hostile land. Like his teacher, he is steadfast in his resolve to share the truth with others who have lost their way.

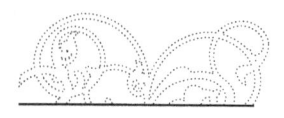

> **Scripture is full of examples of people and prophets who have struggled through enemy attack simply because they followed the One True God.**

The Passage:

Read Matthew 5:11–12. Write down key points from the text and journal your thoughts about what you have read:

_____

_____

_____

The Details:

1. Have you been personally insulted because you were a Christian? If so, how did it make you feel? If not, think about how society talks negatively about Christianity, and how unbelievers try to squelch your ability to pray openly, or to speak about your faith in the workplace, and share how this has affected you:

_____

_____

_____

WEEK THREE

2. Look up 1 Peter 4:4. This verse talks about old acquaintances who don't understand the transformed life of a new believer. Have you had people who didn't accept your Christian morals and godly choices? Have you experienced a time when non-Christians have treated you badly because you "weren't any fun" and wouldn't engage in sinful activities with them? What was your reaction?

_____
_____
_____

3. Jesus assures us that even when others persecute or malign us in any way because we have faith in Him, we will be blessed because of it. Matthew 5:12 reveals where that blessing waits for us—where is it?

_____
_____
_____

4. Matthew 5:12 also mentions that we aren't alone in our persecution. Who else has been persecuted? Why would He end with this statement?

_____
_____
_____

A Closer Look:

We aren't alone in our suffering. God is not surprised by the devil's schemes. Since the Garden of Eden, Satan has been continually employing the same tactics in an attempt to throw the believers of God off their game. Yet, again, in this passage, Jesus teaches the disciples how to live godly lives; we are reminded that we are not alone. Others have suffered. Jesus endured the most suffering. Because of Jesus, our suffering is not in vain. We have a hope, and a promise of eternity. Whether we leave this earth early in our years, or late in our faith walk, the prize is the same for those who trust in the truth of the gospel: our reward is in heaven.

VERSES WE KNOW BY HEART

A Question for Your Life Today:

If owning a Bible instantly became illegal, and you were told to never read Scripture again, what would you do? Would you stand firm in your faith and risk persecution, or would you turn from Almighty God simply because of the laws of man? How does today's lesson help you stand firm?

_____

_____

_____

_____

....

WORKS CITED:

Wiersbe, Warren W.: *Wiersbe's Expository Outlines on the New Testament*. Wheaton, IL: Victor Books, 1997, c1992, S. 27.

Alcorn, Randy: *Safely Home*. Carol Stream, IL: Tyndale House Publishers, 2001. Page 313.

Voice of the Martyrs. www.persecution.com. PO Box 443, Bartlesville, OL 74005-0443. 1-877-337-0302.

Zodhiates, Spiros: *The Complete Word Study Dictionary: New Testament*. Electronic ed. Chattanooga, TN: AMG Publishers, 2000, c1992, c1993, S. G1518.

WEEK FOUR

Seeking the Lord

Wisdom from the Lord's Prayer

Matthew 6:5–13

HELP! It is amazing what four little letters can signify in a moment of desperation and need. Whether Christian or otherwise, everyone has the opportunity to tilt their head toward heaven and whisper, "God, if you're up there, can you help me out with this one?" Prayer is possible for those who seem least likely to pray, or who appear to be quite far from God.

What's wrong with asking for help? On the surface, nothing is wrong with it. The root issue resides deep within the heart of the one who utters the prayer. If the person has no faith in the God of the Bible, the request uttered will float along, and attach to any sort of false impression of a god he has created in his mind— hope clinging hard and fast to an ineffective deity. Those random petitions have no power. Why?

Faith, power, and prayer are a winning combination. Even the person who cries out in desperation and says, "God, if you do this, I'll follow you and believe in Jesus" has hope, because they are showing a sense of faith that Jesus exists. Without any glimpse of faith in the One True God, pagan prayers are nothing but meaningless whispers in the wind.

One of my favorite scenes from Scripture that describes the passionate prayers aimed at false gods is found in the life story of Elijah. In 1 Kings 18 and 19,

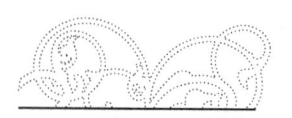

> **Our God is *The God*. Our prayers go to the one place where true answers are found.**

a mountaintop prayer scene of massive proportions occurs when hundreds of false prophets begin dancing around, shouting, pleading, and even mutilating their own flesh in hopes of calling down the power of their false deities. Our God simply waits for them to become weary in their prayers and find that their attempts to call on nothing get them, well, nothing. God has challenged the false gods of man's imagination to a duel of sorts. We can imagine how the story ends. In a victorious display of power, God uses Elijah to call out with one solid prayer, and *whoosh!* God shows up. Victory is won through the mighty authority of the God of all Creation.

What's the moral of that story? Our God is *the* God. Our prayers go to the one place where true answers are found.

In today's world, we can find a multitude of false prayer avenues. Our communities are filled with well-meaning "good" people who have placed their trust in gods who cannot answer. Without a connection to the One with the power to provide answers, those prayers literally fall on deaf ears. These same "spiritual" people will try to convince us that our God is really no more special than their god—that we all follow the same divine presence that goes by different names. Friend, don't be deceived. Our God is different. Our prayers are different. It is His Power receiving our requests that makes our prayers effective.

But prayer is more than asking for help!

It is our communication with the Godhead.

It is our conduit for building relationship with the Father.

It is our conversation with our Savior.

In this week's journey, we will discover how Jesus told His disciples, and the generations since, to pray to the Father. We will learn exactly how to approach our Heavenly Father, and what sorts of things we are to pray about, in light of, and for. God is so much bigger than our temporary needs and troubles. He is our God. And He delights in building relationships with His children, even you and me.

DAY ONE

WEEK FOUR

IMPRESSING MAN OR SEEKING GOD - MATTHEW 6:5–8

The Focus Verse:

And when you pray, do not use vain repetitions as the heathen do. For they think that they will be heard for their many words. **Matthew 6:7, NKJV**

The Main Thought:

God isn't into performance art.

The Story within the Story:

Have you ever heard someone praying a public prayer who obviously was more captivated with his own words than with the recipient of the prayer? Trust me, it happens. Just like Elijah's mob on the mountaintop, anyone can get caught up in performing public prayers for personal gain. It's tragic to watch, really. I vividly remember a day when this scene played out in my own life story.

My husband and I had just nestled into our assigned seats at a community luncheon. Our salads were already positioned in the center of our table setting, surrounded by the accessories for the meal to come: silverware, napkins, glassware, and condiments. The paper program for the event was neatly placed next to each person's napkin, and we could see that we were in for a treat with a distinguished guest delivering the prayer. As the event began, the lights dimmed slightly and the attendees were asked to bow their heads for the invocation. The time had come for the blessing of the meal.

Our notable pray-er was invited up to the podium to pray the blessing over the meal. He looked the part, formal and dignified. It seemed as though he was surrounded by a cloud of spirituality, one he clearly hoped conveyed an intimacy with his god than surpassed what anyone else could ever achieve. As he stepped up to the microphone and drew in a long breath, the spiritual leader began his monologue. Heads bowed and hands folded, the crowd joined him in a moment of reflection as they listened to his prayer. Rather than an expression of desire for God or his blessings, this well-planned performance was more of a poetry reading.

VERSES WE KNOW BY HEART

After what seemed like hours, the speaker stopped his speech as dramatically as he began. He failed to acknowledge who or what He was praying to, and certainly never prayed in anyone's name. As the lights grew brighter once more, a few in the crowd clapped. *They applauded his prayer!* I shuddered and slid down an inch in my chair, embarrassed for the crowd as they missed the point of an invocation altogether. The response of the multitude was proof that the prayer had been much more about the man behind the words than about the God who should have been their focus.

That situation serves as a powerful lesson to all of us. It doesn't matter how spiritual we seem or how much the crowd likes to hear us talk. When we pray, it isn't performance art. It is communication with God.

The Passage:

Read Matthew 6:5–8. Write down key points from the text and journal your thoughts about what you have read:

_____

_____

_____

The Details:

1. Matthew 6:5 warns against praying like the hypocrites. How are hypocritical prayers described in this verse?

_____

_____

_____

2. When do those people receive the reward (or benefit) for their prayers? Why doesn't God bless them beyond this type of show?

_____

_____

WEEK FOUR

3. Does verse 6 mean we need to go into a literal closet to pray? What does this concept convey to us as a people who communicate with God? What is the point of the "closet" idea?

_____
_____
_____

4. Matthew 6:7 talks about meaningless repetition. Where have you seen this method used in religious traditions around the world, and why is that ineffective when seeking coherent communication with God?

_____
_____
_____

5. According to verse 8, when does God know our needs? Is it the eloquence of our words or the genuineness of our heart that makes God listen to our pleas?

_____
_____
_____

A Closer Look:

In Luke's Gospel account, the Lord's Prayer (Luke 11:1–8) begins with a request from a disciple. The follower wants Jesus to teach the disciples how to pray. Just as they had been taught by John the Baptist, these disciples of Christ wanted to receive useful instruction from their new teacher. What Jesus expressed through the answer—what we now know as the Lord's Prayer—is certainly not meant to be a memorized poem we recite back to God on a daily basis. It is the key—a lifeline—into understanding who God is, and how He desires us to come before Him in communication. The prayer Jesus taught the disciples gave them, and us, a pathway to understanding a deeper relationship with the Father.

VERSES WE KNOW BY HEART

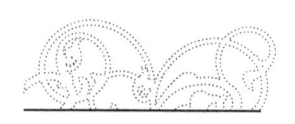

"Lord, teach us to pray . . ." (Luke 11:1).

We've learned today that God isn't impressed with our long-winded monologues and fancy vocabularies. He isn't seeking a people who will chant meaningless phrases over and over in an attempt to find a deeper spiritual union with "the divine." God knows our hearts, and our needs. He wants us to come before Him as a child seeks out the help of his father. Abba Father wants us to call on him with sincerity, a pure heart, and genuine trust that He will provide what He thinks is best for His children.

A Question for Your Life Today:

What do your prayers sound like? Are you a poetic performer when talking to God, or are you more concerned with authentic communication between believer and Lord? Describe your prayer tone, and how you can intentionally form more realistic prayers to God:

_____

_____

_____

DAY TWO

GOD FIRST - MATTHEW 6:9–10

The Focus Verse:

Our Father, who is in heaven, hallowed be Your name. Matthew 6:9

The Main Thought:

God is holy.

WEEK FOUR

The Story within the Story:

During a trip to Africa, I witnessed a cultural example of what it means to address the leader of a people before any other requests can be made. Our group arrived at our destination early in the evening, and spent that first night unpacking, visiting with our colleagues, and enjoying a home cooked meal.

First thing the next morning, before any other desired ministry activities could take place, our hosts explained that we would have to go see the king. Before we would be free to roam the desert region, the king needed to be aware of our presence. He was our priority. So we dressed in appropriate clothing and hopped in the truck.

Leaving the house, we noticed a man standing by the property gate. He was a city official who had come to find out why these foreigners had come to the city. Our host simply looked at the authorities with a firm resolve and exclaimed, "We're going to see *the king*. You'll just have to wait until we get back." The driver pressed the gas pedal, we chugged forward, and the guard swiftly closed the gate behind us. Off we went, down the dusty road to the king's compound.

Driving to the palace, we reviewed the cultural rules of communication with the host. *Say this, don't say that. These are the appropriate gestures and body language. These are the restrictions while at the king's palace.* We had to be sure that we approached the king with reverence, and acknowledged his position of authority over the kingdom and over our visit to his territory. Only after we'd spent time in fellowship, hospitality, and showing due respect, could we complete the rest of our purpose for that mission.

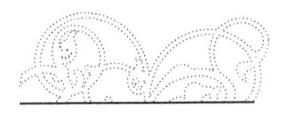

How much more shall we, as followers of the King of kings and Lord of lords, make Jesus our priority and acknowledge His place of authority in our lives?

The Passage:

Read Matthew 6:9–10. Write down key points from the text and journal your thoughts about what you have read:

_____

_____

_____

The Details:

1. As we begin our journey in the Lord's Prayer, what is the very first thing we do, according to Matthew 6:9? Where is God, and why does Jesus make a point of stating the Lord's position and authority before anything else?

VERSES WE KNOW BY HEART

_____
_____
_____

The second half of the verse talks about God's name. How is His name different from other names?

_____
_____
_____

"My mouth will speak the praise of the Lord; and all flesh will bless His holy name forever and ever" (Psalm 145:21).

2. Beginning the Lord's Prayer with God and His position means we begin with worship. Why is it important to focus on worshiping God before we pray through our wants, needs, and requests?

_____
_____
_____

3. Read 1 Samuel 2:1–2. It gives us another example of worshiping through prayer and praise. What does Hannah sing in worship to God? How did she acknowledge His holiness and position as Lord?

_____
_____
_____

4. Returning to Matthew 6, let's think about the phrase "the kingdom of God." The kingdom of God is found within the heart of the believer. In light of this, why would we want to see God's kingdom come as we are praying, and why would Jesus connect that thought to the idea of God's will being done "on earth as it is in heaven?"

_____
_____

WEEK FOUR

A Closer Look:

The Greek term for "hallowed," **hagiázō**, is defined in this way:

> to regard and venerate as holy, to hallow (Mattew 6:9; Luke 11:2; 1 Peter 3:15 . . .). Thus the verb **hagiázō**, to sanctify, when its object is something that is filthy or common, can only be accomplished by separation (**aphorízō** [873]) or withdrawal. It also refers to the withdrawal from fellowship with the world and selfishness by gaining fellowship with God.[a]

Separating ourselves from the selfish desires of the world, and trading those old connections in for a brand new affiliation with God? What a great idea! When talking about the right attitudes of prayer, I think it's interesting to note that the first thing we have to do is acknowledge that the Lord isn't just another man-made illusion of deity. The truth about God becomes our foundation. He's set apart from the world, and holy. He's in heaven, and we are to honor and glorify Him through a right perspective of Him.

Along with regarding His name as holy, we also need to understand that our prayers are effective when we are looking for *God's will*. Sure, we can ask for anything we want, but God is only obligated to do what is within His sovereign plan for the circumstance. We have a choice, but life always goes smoother when we choose the wisdom of God over the wisdom of man. So, if it's effectual prayers we're looking for, this passage gives us great insight on how to make that happen. We've got to want our desires and decisions to line up with God's will. In doing so, our prayers will reflect His kingdom agenda, and we'll be obedient followers of the Lord, able to deal with any situation in the strength and peace of the Lord.

A Question for Your Life Today:

Do you make scheduled visits with God through prayer? Are these visits a priority, and are they at the top of your "to do" list? Most importantly, is worship the primary focus of your prayer time?

VERSES WE KNOW BY HEART

DAY THREE

GOD'S PROVISION - MATTHEW 6:11

The Focus Verse:

Give us this day our daily bread. **Matthew 6:11**

The Main Thought:

God will sustain us.

The Story within the Story:

Journey back through time with me, and let's think about the nation of Israel as they fled their captors in Egypt. When the Lord brought the Israelites out of their chains and into the wilderness, He provided for their daily needs in a variety of ways. He performed miracles leading to their freedom, including the parting of bodies of water as escape routes. God knew exactly how to bring forth victory for His people. Moses, the chosen leader, obediently trailed behind God's lead each day—following His pillar of cloud in the day and pillar of fire at night. God became the perfect GPS (God Provides Solutions) system for the Israelites!

Beyond travel directions and deliverance from evil, the Lord provided for the physical needs of His people through the provision of water and daily food. The manna that fell from heaven each day was exactly what the people needed, in the exact measure. One day at a time, the followers of God had satisfied tummies and safe travels (Exodus 16:13–19).

Imagine the desperation those same people would have felt had they not had daily provision from God: a constant fear of starving would have consumed their every

WEEK FOUR

moment. Yet through the tremendous favor of the Lord, they were full and healthy. The Lord provided daily bread for the Israelites thousands of years ago, and He cares just as much about us today. What is your daily need? What provisions are essential for your survival?

Trust that the Lord will sustain you.

Ask Him to provide.

Be careful though, an ungrateful heart will bring forth the correction of the Lord! Remember what happened when the Israelites got tired of eating manna? When the travelers wanted a variety of menu choices? They got what they wanted, but it wound up being a curse instead of a blessing. God gave the people quail to eat, but "while the meat was still between their teeth, before it was chewed, the anger of the Lord was kindled against the people, and the Lord struck the people with a very severe plague" (Numbers 12:33). Let's be sure to ask for what we need, and not risk getting trapped in the snares of things we want.

The Passage:

Read Matthew 6:11. Write down key points from the text and journal your thoughts about what you have read:

_____

_____

_____

The Details:

1. Read Exodus 16:13–21. God provided daily manna from heaven, but what happened when they tried to store extra amounts?

_____

_____

_____

VERSES WE KNOW BY HEART

2. Today's verse starts out with the phrase "give us this day." As we think about the story of the manna, how does it relate to our need for a regular prayer life? Will one day of praying meet our need for communication with God for a lifetime? What happens to those "stale" prayers of yesteryear?

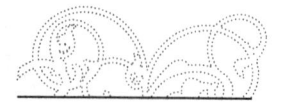

_____

_____

_____

"I am the bread of life" (John 6:48).

3. Read John 6:31–35. In this passage, Jesus explains God's provision of bread from heaven. Who is the bread of life? How does this explain our need to pray for "daily bread"?

_____

_____

_____

A Closer Look:

Wiersbe compares Jesus to the manna in the wilderness in the following ways:

(1) It came from heaven at night; Christ came from heaven when men were in darkness.

(2) It fell on the dew; Christ came, born of the Spirit of God.

(3) It was not defiled by the earth; Christ was sinless, separate from sinners.

(4) It was small, round, and white, suggesting His humility, eternality, and purity.

(5) It was sweet to the taste; Christ is sweet to those who trust Him.

(6) It had to be taken and eaten; Christ must be received and appropriated by faith (1:12–13).

(7) It came as a free gift; Christ is the free gift of God to the world.

(8) There was sufficient for all; Christ is sufficient for all.

(9) If you did not pick it up, you walked on it; if you do not receive Christ, you reject Him and walk on Him (see Hebrews 10:26–31).

(10) It was wilderness food; Christ is our food in this pilgrim journey to heaven.[b]

Jesus's explanation of His role as the bread of life is a fascinating glimpse at just one aspect of our incredible relationship with our Savior. The Father is not a God far off or uninvolved. He has given us an abiding connection with Father, Son, and Holy Spirit that sustains us in our needs. He provides before we know we need provision. The best thing about His daily abundance is: we can ask for it!

A Question for Your Life Today:

Do you trust God to meet your basic needs? How do you incorporate this trust into your communication with the Lord? Do you articulate your needs in prayer?

_____

_____

_____

DAY FOUR

THE TWO SIDES OF FORGIVENESS - MATTHEW 6:12

The Focus Verse:

And forgive us our debts, as we also have forgiven our debtors. Matthew 6:12

The Main Thought:

Forgiveness is a two-way street.

The Story within the Story:

I was late for an appointment. Those who know me understand that being challenged by the clock is a condition that befalls me from time to time, usually as a result of "one-more-thing-itis"—when I mistakenly think I can cram an additional task into an already jam-packed day. Let's just say I'd do well in a culture that was less tied to the minutes in a day, and more focused on relationships. Maybe that's why I do so well on the mission field in Latin and South America.

At any rate, traveling down the highway watching the clock with one eye, and the road with the other, I was shaken right out of my preoccupation with time ticking away when a car zipped out in front of me, causing me to slam on the brakes and pray that we wouldn't smash bumpers. Within seconds it was clear that the only result of his negligent move was a screeching tire or two. It would have been easy for me to yell, or at least give a mean look in his direction. I could have written his license plate number down and called him into the cops. The list of road rage expressions that were available to me are better left to the imagination; but suffice it to say, instead of raging I chose the higher road. After the initial heart palpitation, panicked thought, and foot movements, I simply went about my way, driving to the appointment.

Why not get mad at the guy, instead of brushing it off? The main reason is the fact that I know others have extended me the same forgiveness. We've all done it; at some point in our driving experience we've pulled out in front of somebody by mistake, or almost missed a turn and jerked the car without looking behind us. Haven't you almost bumped into another car because a blind spot totally hid them from view? I know that I've been in his shoes, so why not forgive as I've been forgiven? Besides, I had an appointment to get to. No time to waste.

The Passage:

Read Matthew 6:12. Write down key points from the text and journal your thoughts about what you have read:

_____

_____

_____

WEEK FOUR

The Details:

1. The term "debts" in Matthew 6:12 deals with more than financial amounts owed. It also speaks of any offense, moral or otherwise. Look up Luke 11:4, and write out the first part of the verse. What key word is different from Matthew 6:12?

_____

_____

_____

Which is harder for you to forgive: someone's financial debt to you, or a moral breach of trust or integrity shortfall? Why?

_____

_____

_____

2. Looking closer at this verse, we are praying that God will forgive us as we have forgiven others. Think about God's mercy in your life, especially His forgiveness of sin that provided your salvation. How does this effect your desire to forgive others? Does it make you want to be more forgiving?

_____

_____

_____

3. Why do you think Jesus added this element to the prayer He modeled for the disciples?

_____

_____

_____

A Closer Look:

Forgiveness. We could talk about death row inmates who have committed atrocious wrongs in our society. We could think about the nastiest workplace backstabbing and competition. We would be justified in thinking about hurt relationships, broken marriages, abuse and neglect. But let's get straight to the point. Jesus came to earth, fully God yet fully man, in order to be the atoning sacrifice for our sin. We talked about that truth in the first chapter of this book, and our lives will be spent living out the loving grace of the effects of this truth. He came to forgive.

Today, right this moment, let's dwell on the magnitude of the forgiveness that was extended at Calvary:

- For your sin.
- For my sin.
- For the death row inmate.
- For the workplace bully.
- For the adulterous spouse.
- For the predator.
- For the abuser.
- For the forgotten.
- For all sin.

Forgiveness has been extended to all who will accept it. Even to the worst of sinners. Nothing is too tough for God, and no one is so far entrenched in sin that the Lord can't grab them up by their bootstraps and set them on the solid rock of forgiveness. All we have to do is repent, lay those sins at the foot of that cross, believe that Jesus is the Son of God, and live transformed lives of faith. That's what being saved by faith through grace is all about (Ephesians 2:8). So, with that in mind, let's jump back into today's lesson. If God in His great wisdom and love has the patience, power, and energy to forgive all of us, why can't we take some time to forgive those who've hurt us as well?

I know, it's much easier said than done. You're right. I don't know what they've done to you. I wasn't there when it happened. I'm sure the world has told you that you have every "right" to be mad and hold a grudge. I have my own stuff I've had to work through over the years, and a bunch of hidden unforgiveness that the Lord is still pulling out of the depths of my being. But we all have to make a conscious decision to let God deal with those people who have hurt us. He is the Judge of all. Our job is to stop controlling the situation through our unwillingness to forgive, and allow God to bring peace to our hearts through the power of forgiveness. Looking at this week's model prayer, forgiveness is a two-way street. He is faithful to forgive us, and He'll help us do the same for others.

A Question for Your Life Today:

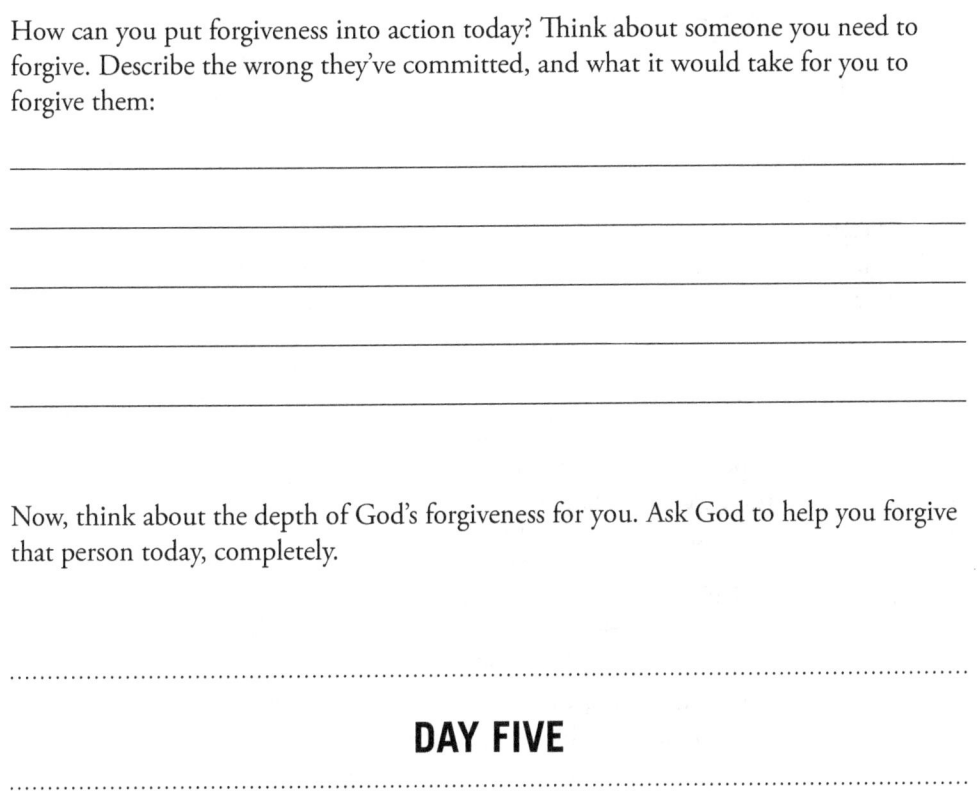

How can you put forgiveness into action today? Think about someone you need to forgive. Describe the wrong they've committed, and what it would take for you to forgive them:

_____

_____

_____

_____

Make today the day you put forgiveness into action!

Now, think about the depth of God's forgiveness for you. Ask God to help you forgive that person today, completely.

DAY FIVE

NO TEMPTATION PLEASE! - MATTHEW 6:13

The Focus Verse:

And do not lead us into temptation, but deliver us from evil. For Thine is the kingdom, and the power, and the glory, forever. Amen. **Matthew 6:13**

The Main Thought:

Beware the temptation trap.

VERSES WE KNOW BY HEART

The Story within the Story:

When pondering the trials of temptation, the first enticement that comes to my mind is chocolate. Oh, yes, the alluring loveliness of cocoa perfection. All it takes is one harsh word, or boredom, or happiness, or grief, or stress, or a special occasion, and our friend the familiar choco-persuasion is waved in front of us like a flag of bondage camouflaged as freedom. Wrap it in a bright red, heart-shaped box, and it's called love. Hide it in a plastic egg, and it's called a springtime treasure hunt. Answer the doorbell, and stick it in a kid's sack, and it's called a treat. Dump it in a mantel piece stocking, and it's a sign you've been good all year. Pay too much for it, and it's called a school fundraiser. Freeze it in a container with ice cream and it's just plain wonderful. In every case, it's hard to resist. Temptation is like that, isn't it?

God is not the cause of our compromise, or the reason for our pattern of temptation in life. He isn't the one wagging the candy wrapper under our nose, or force-feeding it to us in a moment of weakness. The Lord isn't the Boogie Monster lurking behind every doorway, waiting to pounce on unsuspecting humans so He can shove chocolate bars in their mouths. His heart would have us live a life free from the snares of our fleshly desires, but we have to do our part in resisting the carnal nature of the flesh.

Chocolate not your vice? No matter. Whatever the luring scenario, the progression is the same. Sure, we can have a little bit. Yeah, we'll resist it later today, or the next day. Then, before we know it, we've compromised to enticement again, and we're more indebted to the temptation ogre. Just think about some other self-imposed battles we face in life. God doesn't force us to flirt with another person's spouse until we make a tragically wrong choice based on lust and desire. The Lord isn't the one who pulls the slot machine lever after we've already gambled all the mortgage money. He doesn't make us buy that great sale item that doesn't really fit anyway, even when our credit cards are maxed out on a lifetime of good deals. All these things are our own doing, fueled by unbridled desires that were never stopped in their tracks. How do we avoid enticement? Let's look at today's verse and find out.

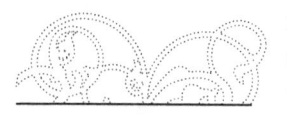

> **God is not the cause of our compromise.**

The Passage:

Read Matthew 6:13. Write down key points from the text and journal your thoughts about what you have read:

_____

_____

The Details:

1. When you read this model prayer taught by Jesus, how does it give you a clue into the ways God wants to help us out in our daily lives?

With that in mind, is He interested in keeping us away from temptation? How can you have confidence that the Lord will protect you from evil?

2. Look at 1 Corinthians 10:13. What does this verse tell you about the regular temptations you face in life?

God is faithful and He also provides a way of escape.

VERSES WE KNOW BY HEART

3. Read James 1:13–14. What does James say about God and temptation? While the Lord will test our faith, He will not cause us to sin. How does this verse confirm this truth?

_____

_____

_____

_____

James explains the progression from temptation to sin as someone being carried away and enticed by *his own* lust. It is our doing, not the Lord's, that gets us in so much trouble!

3. As this verse closes the Lord's Prayer, the New American Standard Bible includes a closing thought in brackets. The New King James Version also adds the phrase. What does that final addition say, and why do you think it is added as a final note to the prayer?

_____

_____

_____

_____

A Closer Look:

The end of Matthew 6:13 reminds us that it is through God's kingdom, and power, and glory that we are victorious. Only He brings forth provision, protection, and forgiveness. How long can we count on this power? For ever and ever. What does this have to do with our prayer life? Everything!

As we finish out this powerful week of learning about effective prayer, we have confidence in knowing that temptation is no match for the power of God. He can deliver us from evil, and from the schemes of the enemy; he will provide a way for us to escape the lure of temptation. But we've got to do our part and remain focused on Him and His will for our lives.

A Question for Your Life Today:

When faced with tempting thoughts, activities, or situations, how do you find the strength to say no? Do you conquer the struggle solely through your own willpower, or do you rely on God's delivering power to rescue you?

_____

_____

_____

_____

_____

WORKS CITED:

Zodhiates, Spiros: *The Complete Word Study Dictionary: New Testament*. Electronic ed. Chattanooga, TN: AMG Publishers, 2000, c1992, c1993, S. G37.

Wiersbe, Warren W.: *Wiersbe's Expository Outlines on the New Testament*. Wheaton, IL: Victor Books, 1997, c1992, S. 227.

VERSES WE KNOW BY HEART

WEEK FIVE

The True Meaning of Love

God's Love Passage

1 Corinthians 12:31–13:13

Something old and something new, something borrowed and something blue. These traditional additions to our culture's wedding ceremonies could include a handkerchief, an old string of pearls, a trinket, and a treasure. Whatever items combine to make the bride's completion of the custom, the old, new, borrowed, and blue categories of our life are ones we hold quite dear. But wedding days are made of more than rhymes like these; we also make promises before God and harbor hopes and dreams of a happily-ever-after.

As with my own nuptial ceremony, many church wedding services include the passage we'll study this week: 1 Corinthians 13. It isn't difficult to call to mind the memory of my pastor reading these words from his Bible. I can almost feel the presence of my family around me and my husband's eyes gazing into mine as the truth of a godly love was read, just before our vows were taken. How fitting to hear what God has to say about love as we commit to loving another person until death do us part. But is this chapter of the Bible really focused on weddings, or love?

VERSES WE KNOW BY HEART

Love. An unassuming little word with more meaning than it could ever imply. We long to be loved. We commit to loving others. God, out of His great love for us, provided a path to restored relationship with Him. And, in this letter to the Corinthians, Paul uses the topic of love to describe a "more excellent way" of life. Paul's inclusion of this issue in his letter to the church does not derive from a need to facilitate wedding ceremonies; he has the health of the body of believers in mind. Paul longs to see the rambunctious church in Corinth loving more, and striving for spiritual sportsmanship less. He wants their motivations pure, and their hearts dedicated to glorifying God—not focused on man's ability to dynamically communicate.

DAY ONE

A MORE EXCELLENT WAY - 1 CORINTHIANS 12:31–13:13

The Focus Verse:

...and I show you a still more excellent way. **1 Corinthians 12:31**

The Main Thought:

God's love is the foundation of living an excellent life.

The Story within the Story:

Every autumn, families around our country begin filling empty shoe boxes full of toys, treasures, and candies. Festive wrapping paper adorns the outside, and a special gift tag is affixed to the lid. Prayers are spoken over each container with the needs and hopes of the recipient in mind. After being delivered to a local collection point, these boxes of wonder are collected and sent to a large distribution center. From there, the gifts aplenty travel in larger boxes to distant lands where children receive what might possibly be their only gift all year.

WEEK FIVE

Wrapped in love, the presents travel a world away. Filled with tidings of good wishes and the message of hope found in Jesus Christ, the gifts are much more than a bunch of toys crammed in a decorated box. Love fills each container. God's love is felt by each set of tiny hands that opens their Christmas gift. Across desert expanses, rainforest communities, and mountain villages, joy bursts forth. The kids so far away aren't only excited to receive a special gift; they are also amazed that a complete stranger took the time to show the love of Christ to them in a tangible way. The givers are motivated, even compelled, by the love of Jesus.

When thinking about this week's passage, and our first day's focus on "a more excellent way," the shoe box ministry came to mind right away. Our family has supported this ministry in a variety of ways over the years, and we've seen and heard what a difference it makes in the lives of others. This worldwide effort organized by Operation Christmas Child[a] makes an impact for the kingdom of God. It shares Jesus with the nations. It blesses those who go without. It draws the love of Jesus out of the body of believers, and compels them to show a more excellent love than the world can understand.

The Passage:

Read 1 Corinthians 12:31–13:13. Write down key points from the text and journal your thoughts about what you have read:

_____

_____

_____

"Now there are varieties of gifts, but the same Spirit" (1 Corinthians 12:4).

The Details:

1. This week's passage is better understood in light of the previous chapter on spiritual gifts. Read 1 Corinthians 12. Why does God equip us with special gifts and abilities?

_____

_____

_____

VERSES WE KNOW BY HEART

2. Do we all have the same gifts, or are we uniquely equipped to build up the entire body of Christ? Explain:

___

___

___

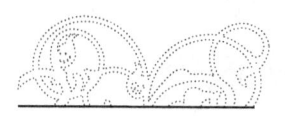

> "But to each one is given the manifestation of the Spirit for the common good" (1 Corinthians 12:7).

3. With our gifts and the purpose of our gifts in mind, now look at the passage for this week. Why is love so important when thinking about building others up in their faith and working together?

___

___

___

4. Why do you think Paul structured his letter to the Corinthians like this? Why was it so important for the church to understand the concept of love partnered with gifts?

___

___

___

A Closer Look:

Tucked into Scripture, between the description of spiritual gifts and the implementation of some of those gifts, lies an explanation of love that involves using our lives to glorify God. Our goal is to focus on loving others as God loves us rather than scouting out whatever God might give us that could make us look super spiritual. But beyond gifts, we will understand through our studies this week that the love spoken of in 1 Corinthians is given by God, and tapped into by the people of God.

Warren Wiersbe states the following with regard to our focus passage of 1 Corinthians 13:

WEEK FIVE

It is tragic when the world takes a chapter like this (as it does) and divorces it from its true Christian meaning. The unsaved man can no more experience this kind of love than can a marble statue! It takes the indwelling of the Spirit of God in the life, and the empowering of that Spirit, for anyone to display this kind of character in daily life.

A Question for Your Life Today:

Do you know what spiritual gifts God has equipped you with? If so, list them here. If not, commit to studying about spiritual gifts, and tapping into who God has created you to be in Him!

_____

_____

_____

_____

A good resource for discovering your spiritual gifts is *Spiritual Gifts: A Practical Guide to How God Works Through You* by David Francis.

DAY TWO

GIFTS, OR THE GIFT OF LOVE? - 1 CORINTHIANS 13:1–3

The Focus Verse:

If I speak with the tongues of men and of angels, but do not have love, I have become a noisy gong or a clanging cymbal. **1 Corinthians 13:1**

The Main Thought:

Don't settle for life as a clanging cymbal.

VERSES WE KNOW BY HEART

The Story within the Story:

I love watching a skilled orchestra play the classic works of days gone by. With precise notes and perfect pitch, each note of genius flows through the air because a large team of workers manipulate instruments of wood, metal, and string in the exact manner in which they were designed to operate. From one group's introduction of the beginning of the piece, to the weaving in and out of other layers of music, each part of that orchestra knows when to play, when to rest, and when to watch the conductor for instruction. It's fascinating.

One of my favorite pieces of symphonic music is used for fireworks accompaniment and patriotic events. As the air jets through the brass section's instruments, pumping out sounds of a famous composition, the wind instruments and percussion jump in and out of the parade-style music, motivating the crowd to march around a field in celebration. The music inspires and uplifts, full of life.

Somewhere in that familiar tune we know the music will incorporate a surprising twist. You know: the clash of the cymbals. At just the right moment the brass saucers will collide, making a huge sound in the middle of our song. We expect it, but each time it takes us almost by surprise. Out of nowhere comes the *crash bang*, and then almost as quickly as it shocks, it's out of the song again—until the next time it is needed for effect. An interesting thing about the cymbals; they don't carry a melody or change notes. The discs just clang together in one loud crash of impact. They cannot play a tune on their own; they just startle the rest of the song with a monotone impact of brass on brass. Even still, there's nothing like a perfectly timed yet very brief appearance by the cymbals to make music come alive.

But what about the poor cymbal player who gets his timing wrong? What if, in the midst of the lull in the song, a huge *crash, bang, clank* came from the back of the symphony orchestra? What if the percussion player missed his timing, and became a symbol of confusion instead of a cymbal of musical perfection? Worse yet: what if he felt so irritated that his part in the music was insignificant, that he clanged more, whether it was in the sheet music or not? It would be awful. We'd be hard pressed to remember it for long, unless, of course, we reflected on how absurd the whole moment in time had become. The song never would have reached the full potential intended because someone operated outside the boundaries of instruction.

Think about our spiritual gifts and love. If we're so set on clanging and gathering attention for ourselves through dynamic displays of spirituality, what will it sound like in the midst of a symphony of believers who are working together without us? As we clang to our own beat, we will miss out on hitting the perfectly timed notes God has called us to play. We will sound out of touch and out of sync with what God is doing in the world. A cymbal that steps out of God's timing is fueled not by love, but by pride. The clang you will hear is nothing but a "look at me" moment in a "called to look at God" Christian lifestyle. Such gongs and cymbals are not fondly remembered.

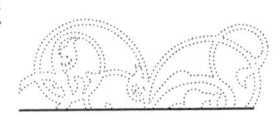

> As we clang to our own beat, we miss out on hitting the perfectly timed notes God has called us to play.

The Passage:

Read 1 Corinthians 13:1–3. Write down key points from the text and journal your thoughts about what you have read:

___

The Details:

1. If we take 1 Corinthians 13:1–2 simply as a discussion of eloquence and communication superiority, is great speech and verbal connection *enough* when we're reaching out to others? What else do we need in order to be effective in showing the love of God?

___

2. According to verse 1, what do our special words sound like if they aren't fueled by love?

___

While a clanging cymbal or a noisy gong may make a shockingly loud sound that startles the listener for a moment, the message they send is more fleeting and harsh. Our goal should be to produce a soothing, lasting, effective love of God shared with a hurting world.

3. Verse 2 mentions knowledge, wisdom, prophecy, and faith. Such things bring great impact, but without love, what significance do they have?

_____

_____

_____

Without love, wisdom and knowledge are nothing.

4. 1 Corinthians 13:3 talks about suffering for a spiritual cause and helping the poor. What types of suffering for Christ, or self-sacrifice in order to help the needy, have you heard about in our generation?

_____

_____

_____

5. Without love and the right heart attitude, what good does it do to feed the poor or go through extreme measures to look spiritual? While the hungry are fed, and we may look dedicated, what does God say about our actions?

_____

_____

_____

A Closer Look:

Without love as our foundation, all our efforts to impact the world by using the spiritual gifts the Lord has given will be a waste of time. The ways the Lord equips us are not to be ignored or looked down upon. On the contrary, His creative power working through us in order to bring Himself glory should be celebrated. But in the daily working out of our purpose, we should never forget the greatest gift from God—His love.

God's love propels us to use our gifts, and He compels us by His truth to share our faith with the world. The Lord has given us many avenues of communication, all of which are best used when we are extending a voice, heart, and life of compassion to our communities.

A Question for Your Life Today:

When you talk to unbelievers about Jesus, are you more focused on the particular words you're saying, or the heart attitude in which you deliver your message? Which is more important to God?

___

___

___

DAY THREE

LOVE IS . . . - 1 CORINTHIANS 13:4–5

The Focus Verse:

Love is patient, love is kind . . . 1 Corinthians 13:4

The Main Thought:

Love keeps the best interest of others in mind.

The Story within the Story:

O. Henry's classic story, *The Gift of the Magi*, has intrigued my heart for a lifetime. The classic tale, however brief, impacts the mind of the reader as the issue of giving the perfect Christmas gift is explored. Two people, joined together in love, admiration, and wedding vows, are surviving on a tight budget. A small amount of money scraped together in the wife's hand makes for a creative decision.

The most striking physical feature of this woman, named Della, is her beautiful long hair. She goes to the hair goods dealer and attempts to sell her hair; to have her greatest treasure cut off and taken away. Twenty dollars later, the long-haired wife has become a short-haired consumer, searching the store windows for the perfect gift: a watch chain. Why is that the perfect gift? Just as her mane is her beauty, her husband's gold watch is a family heirloom and his pride and joy. What bliss she experiences as she rushes home with what she considers the perfect gift. Once she settles in at their domicile, she focuses on making her trimmed mop of hair as pretty as she can before her love returns home. In the midst of her desperate curling and styling, her heart cries out in hopes that her husband will still love her without her trademark locks.

On the flip side of this account of selfless generosity is the husband, who waltzes in the door after a long day at work. He stares at her, and her lack of tresses, with the strangest expression. He finally embraces her with a sweet understanding of the depth of her love for him as proved through her sacrifice. Then he gives his bride her Christmas gift: hair combs. The pair she longed to have! Only now, there was no place to secure those combs on her head. The moment becomes ever more sweet as she hands him his sparkling new chain; the one that would have fit perfectly on his watch. This gift was, after all, the motivation for her short hairdo. The only problem is, he sold that heirloom to purchase her hair combs. Both had intended on lavishing love on the other with a gift. The real gift became their selfless acts of love.

Together they celebrated the holiday. Despite the sacrifice they'd each made on behalf of the other, they were cheerful and full of adoration for one another. It wasn't about the presents, but the love they demonstrated. Mr. and Mrs. James Dillingham Young learned the concept of sacrificial giving, much as the magi of the days of Jesus's birth understood the greatest treasure of their day was the Savior sent in love by the Father.

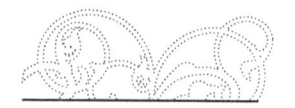

It wasn't about the presents, but the love they demonstrated.

The Passage:

Read 1 Corinthians 13:4–5. Write down key points from the text and journal your thoughts about what you have read:

_____

_____

_____

The Details:

1. What are the positive qualities of love, as mentioned in 1 Corinthians 13:4–5? What does love do?

2. What are the things that love does *not* do?

How do these aspects of love, when applied to our lives, change how we interact with people? What happens to our relationships if we don't remain within these boundaries of love?

3. Patience, kindness, forgiveness, humility, and peacefulness all reflect a commitment to godliness. We'll look at Galatians 5:22–23 and the fruit of the spirit next week, but for now, how do you think these qualities bring forth godliness?

VERSES WE KNOW BY HEART

4. What does 2 Thessalonians 5:14 tell us about how to love others?

_____

_____

A Closer Look:

The short story about Christmas gifts coupled with today's lesson on the virtues of Christian love leads us to a deeper understanding of godly love. It isn't just an outward expression. It isn't fueled by our needs. It isn't rooted in emotion. True love, according to the Father, is an abiding relationship with God and others that exhibits the qualities and principles that God exhibits. Those who love trust the God who *is* love. The genuine love of the Lord seeks the best interest of others.

A Question for Your Life Today:

In what ways can you show godly love to family members? What types of selfless service and benevolence can you implement this week?

_____

_____

_____

DAY FOUR

LOVE PROTECTS - 1 CORINTHIANS 13:6–7

The Focus Verse:

[Love] does not rejoice in unrighteousness, but rejoices with the truth.
1 Corinthians 13:6 (brackets my addition)

WEEK FIVE

The Main Thought:

Love seeks the truth.

The Story within the Story:

"La verdad, Mama, la verdad" she said with firmness as she walked out of the courtroom.

"No matter what happens, we stand on the truth" she admonished as they sat down together on the hard wood bench in the hallway.

One who once was the love of her life had turned into her chief accuser. Years of trouble had culminated in a heap of lawyers' files. The day was difficult, but the worn out woman being dragged through the mud in a court hearing wouldn't stand for unrighteousness. Her firm resolve was focused on the truth. No matter the outcome. To her, this was godly love, even in the sight of persecution. If she was punished for being upright and honest, so be it. But there would be no tolerance of a love of self-interest as shown on the opposite side of the courtroom. She wouldn't even begin to entertain the thought of destroying another person just to avoid further unjust persecution directed at her.

In this situation, this season of life, there would be troubles, but no one could steal her hope, her endurance, and her integrity. She testified about her life for the sake of her future. In this, her love for her children, her family, and her God would prevail as she stood for what was right, no matter what kind of case was built against her. After all, she answers to God, not a vindictive man. She models a godly life for her kids. She stands on the truth. Therefore, she has hope, she bears the struggle, and she resolves to endure.

Witnessing this picture of loving righteousness, I sat at the other end of the bench wondering if I could do the same. Pondering whether I could show such love in an unlovely situation, and whether I would rather rejoice in the thought of unrighteousness, however justified it might have been. Yes. Of course, I would rejoice with her in the truth, regardless of the outcome of the court hearings. Why? This is the heart of God and the heartbeat of those who follow Him.

VERSES WE KNOW BY HEART

The Passage:

Read 1 Corinthians 13:6–7. Write down key points from the text and journal your thoughts about what you have read:

_____
_____
_____

The Details:

1. Like yesterday's lesson, list out the things love does do, according to verses 6 and 7:

_____
_____
_____

2. Now note the things love doesn't do:

_____
_____
_____

3. How do these things compare to yesterday's list? What is the focus of love in today's verses, and how will that affect our relationships and our faith?

_____
_____
_____

4. Think about the terms rejoice, bear, believe, hope, and endure. What do these concepts reveal about the Christian life? If they all connect to love, what is the impact of such qualities active in a believer?

_____

_____

_____

5. Read Job 1:13–22. What happened to Job? What did he lose?

_____

_____

_____

According to verse 22, what was Job's response?

_____

_____

_____

"Through all this Job did not sin nor did he blame God" (Job 1:22).

6. Look up James 5:11. Who is blessed?

_____

_____

_____

What does the end of verse 11 reveal about the impact a person who has endured has as a witness to others? What do we learn about the goodness of God through the lives of people around us?

_____

_____

_____

A Closer Look:

Today we learned that love "rejoices with the truth; bears all things, believes all things, hopes all things, endures all things" (1 Corinthians 13:6–7). When we think about those who have endured trials, like Job, we can stand confident that our God "is full of compassion and is merciful" (James 5:11). We shouldn't blame God for our misfortune, or give up hope that the Lord is with us. Instead, we should look more closely toward God, and seek his presence in that situation. When we live lives infused with the love of Christ, we will be equipped not merely to endure, but to rejoice, hope, believe, and stand strong. Endurance is a long-term concept, and our call to love is unending.

A Question for Your Life Today:

Think about your long-term relationships with family, spouse, and friends. Describe a time where you had to endure a difficult season with a loved one. How did God help you through that time?

_____

_____

_____

DAY FIVE

GREATEST OF THESE - 1 CORINTHIANS 13:8–13

The Focus Verse:

But now abide faith, hope, love, these three; but the greatest of these is love.

1 Corinthians 13:13

WEEK FIVE

The Main Thought:

Love is the most important goal.

The Story within the Story:

"When I grow up, I'm never going to treat my kids like this! You're so unfair!" The words of angst flying out of a teenager's mouth as she stomps up the staircase to her room are all too familiar. In fact, the words are extremely familiar: the words were mine. As I slammed the bedroom door and flopped on my bed, the drama of rules, regulations, and boundaries keeping me from the fun I thought I would rather have consumed every brain cell's attention. I just knew I was the only kid that wasn't allowed to run wild. *Or so I thought.* Looking back on things now, it was those very moments of steadfast rules that protected me from my own poor judgment. Love from two parents who were dedicated to providing a household built on values and truth kept me from even more trouble. I just couldn't see it at the time.

Sometimes we don't understand why our parents reacted in a certain way until we're parents ourselves. Suddenly, with little ones in tow, we gain clarity as to why there are rules and boundaries, set in place by a guardian, intended to keep the child safe. What once sounded like cruel and unusual punishment in a child's ears becomes a wise decision in the mind of an adult. My husband and I have set up our own set of boundaries within our household, all intended to keep our son safe and healthy. I've learned that seasons change, and so do our perspectives on life. As we grow, we understand more about how the world works.

In our spiritual life, we also become transformed more and more over time, reflecting the heart of God in increasing measure as we learn who He is, and who we are in Him. Eventually we come to the realization that less and less of our priorities and motivations focus on us; our lives become more in line with servant leadership principles and others-centered actions. As we mature in our faith, love takes deeper root, and godly love drives our motivations and desires. No longer are our image, reputation, words, or accomplishments the focus—only what the Lord would allow us to do in love is important. God's love is the foundation for our faith, for our hope, and for our life. Our faith is in Jesus, our hope is in eternity, and our love is given to the One who gave all.

> **Our faith is in Jesus, our hope is in eternity, and our love is given to the One who gave all.**

The Passage:

Read 1 Corinthians 13:8–13. Write down key points from the text and journal your

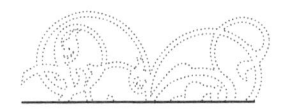

VERSES WE KNOW BY HEART

thoughts about what you have read:

_____
_____
_____

The Details:

1. 1 Corinthians 13:8–10 mentions things that will eventually cease. What is listed?

_____
_____
_____

2. Verse 10 mentions "when the perfect comes"—it is talking about the time we'll be in heaven. Why will we not have to worry about partial knowledge or gifts in heaven?

_____
_____
_____

3. We read in verses 11–12 about the difference between childhood understanding and adulthood, and between a dim mirror versus face-to-face sight. How does this confirm the previous question's point about heaven's full picture?

_____
_____
_____

4. Read 2 Corinthians 3:17–18. What additional information do we find about God's glory, our reflection of that glory, and our transformation in Christ?

_____

WEEK FIVE

_____

_____

_____

5. Go back to 1 Corinthians 13, and read verse 13.

Where do we place our faith?

_____

What do we have a hope in, specifically with regard to salvation?

_____

How do we grow in our ability to love?

_____

_____

We begin our Christian walk by placing our faith in Jesus Christ. Through this relationship we have the hope of glory, the hope of eternal life. As we grow in godliness, we have a greater ability to love!

A Closer Look:

After a week of studying the fine art of love, we see that it literally takes a lifetime to master the skill of loving others. Our walk with the Lord provides continual transformation as we show more compassion, humbly serve others, and trust in the Lord regardless of our circumstances. Today, in our last study of this chapter, we end with the timeless sound byte: "but now abide faith, hope, love, these three; but the greatest of these is love" (1 Corinthians 13:13). Again we confirm the truth that the presence of spiritual gifts is nothing without the compelling force of God's love. *The Bible Knowledge Commentary* reminds us that "the gifts of the Spirit should be controlled by the fruit of the Spirit, chief among which was love (Galatians 5:22)."[d] Next week we'll consider the fruit of the Spirit, and how the outworking of our faith produces fruit that lasts.

A Question for Your Life Today:

What are your new goals concerning loving others? How will you implement the principles learned this week?

....

WORKS CITED:

Operation Christmas Child is a ministry of Samaritan's Purse International Relief. www.samaritanspurse.org. 1-800-353-5957. PO Box 3000, Boone, NC 28607-3000.

Wiersbe, Warren W.: *Wiersbe's Expository Outlines on the New Testament*. Wheaton, IL: Victor Books, 1997, c1992, S. 456.

Henry, O. *Selected Stories of O. Henry.* New York, NY: Barnes and Noble Books, 2003. "*The Gift of the Magi*," pages 25–30.

Walvoord, John F.; Zuck, Roy B.; Dallas Theological Seminary: *The Bible Knowledge Commentary: An Exposition of the Scriptures*. Wheaton, IL: Victor Books, 1983–c1985, S. 2:537.

Francis, David. *Spiritual Gifts: A Practical Guide to How God Works Through You.* Nashville, TN: LifeWay Press, 2003.

WEEK SIX

Making the Perfect Fruit Salad

Fruit of the Spirit

Galatians 5:16–26

Last spring we planted an apple tree: a Granny Smith apple tree. Over the past fourteen months we've watched the plant get established, shoot out new branches, unfurl green leaves, and bring forth dainty white flowers. The beauty of the foliage and blossoms aside, the prize or the *pièce de résistance* is the fruit—the green globes of juicy apple goodness. During the first season we didn't see any apples on our tree. Only the tag's photo gave us hope of its future potential. Sure, we love the beauty of foliage and the majestic growth of the tree itself, but the fruit is what we longed to see.

This year the harvest showed up. After the beauty of the dainty white flowers faded, evidence of apples aplenty emerged. Tiny buds at first, growing into spheres of possibility. A few mini-apples fell off their branches before they ever had a chance to ripen. Fruit that falls early never reaches its full potential. The outside is pretty, but the inside is still bitter. Some of the specimens were beautiful one day, and ridden with worm holes the next. What a pity! The attack left them useless and worn out. Other apples continue to grow, showing promise. But one—one of the green beauties is growing with flair. It's almost ready to be eaten. It's just about ripe. Our mouths water when we inspect the tree and our eyes meet this mighty apple. We just can't wait to taste and see how good the fruit is.

Why the details of this tree? This week we'll be taking a look at the spiritual fruit in our lives. If we don't nurture our spiritual growth, we'll have no fruit to show—we'll be like that apple that fell to the ground, rendered useless and bitter. If we let the woes of the world get to us, we'll be worm-ridden and worn out. If we stay connected to the Holy Spirit, and allow God to guide us through His wisdom in every situation, our reactions to life's challenges will show forth the principles and promises of godly living. We'll have joy, and bring joy to others. We'll be beautiful fruit producers.

DAY ONE

CONTRASTING LIVES - GALATIANS 5:16–26

The Focus Verse:

Now those who belong to Christ Jesus have crucified the flesh with its passions and desires. **Galatians 5:24**

The Main Thought:

God desires us to live holy lives.

The Story within the Story:

Brace yourself. Are you a Christian? If you are, then you're just plain strange according to the politically correct views of our generation. You won't fit in with the trends and traditions of the carnal world, as it tries to justify preferences, actions, and plain old sin as the "healthy" expressions of unique people. Your opinions will not always line up with the political commentary on the nightly news, and your ideas about life, creation of life, marriage, and sexual orientation will be challenged by every liberal communicator in the world. They will ask you questions like "how dare you believe . . . ," and make statements like "don't force on me your religious views about . . ." —yet the critics themselves have no intention of extending to you the same courtesy concerning the ideologies they hold dear, expecting you to endure their views and beliefs.

We are called to stand firm in our faith, living out each day to the glory of God. He calls on us to live holy lives, including living lives that don't bow down to the desires of the flesh. As our focus verse for today reminds us, we have "crucified our flesh" along with Jesus Christ (Galatians 5:24).

Are you standing strong for Jesus in the current crisis of cultural immorality? Even if you've been a believer for years, are you still willing to stand strong against the things that grieve the heart of God? If you are more concerned with being biblically correct than politically correct, trouble's bound to come your way. But God calls on us to react in a godly manner, and make godly choices.

The Passage:

Read Galatians 5:16–26. Write down key points from the text and journal your thoughts about what you have read:

_____

_____

_____

The Details:

1. What does the focus verse mean when it says we have "crucified the flesh"?

_____

_____

_____

2. Read Colossians 2:13–14. What did Jesus nail to the cross?

_____

_____

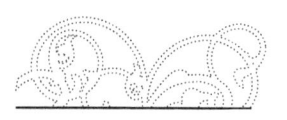

You are a new creation in Christ Jesus.

We sin with our fleshly nature. Jesus has taken our sin and nailed it to the cross, and forgives us the moment we've repented from our sins. When we are reconciled to God through Jesus Christ, we become new creations. 2 Corinthians 5:17 tells us: *"therefore if any man is in Christ, he is a new creature; the old things passed away; behold, new things have come."*

3. With regard to today's passage, how does Galatians 5:16–26 describe a new creation in Christ?

_____

_____

_____

In what ways has your life changed since you've accepted Jesus as Savior? How have you become a "new creation"?

_____

_____

_____

4. Read 1 John 2:15–17. What happens if we love the things of this world? Are they from the Father?

_____

_____

_____

5. What, or who, lasts forever, according to verse 17?

_____

_____

_____

6. In light of this truth, why on earth would we want to focus on fleshly desires?

_____

_____

A Closer Look:

Closing last week's lesson we learned that "the gifts of the Spirit should be controlled by the fruit of the Spirit, chief among which was love (Galatians 5:22)."[a] God's love for us provides salvation. Our repentance opens the door for God's grace and forgiveness. Relationship with Jesus supplies us with the presence and power of the Holy Spirit in the life of the believer. Yet it is our love for Jesus that compels us to share the gifts He has given us through His Spirit. This week we begin with an overview of the passage that helps us control our gifts through the fruit of the Spirit. Which fruit is listed first? You guessed it: love. Once again, love rules the day. Maybe God's trying to tell us something!

A Question for Your Life Today:

How do you avoid the fleshly desires of the world? What are some of your defensive tactics to combat these daily distractions?

_____

_____

_____

DAY TWO

LIVE BY THE SPIRIT - GALATIANS 5:16

The Focus Verse:

But I say, walk by the Spirit, and you will not carry out the desire of the flesh. Galatians 5:16

The Main Thought:

Focusing on God avoids sin.

The Story within the Story:

Grocery shopping can be dangerous work! I've become quite the veteran shopper, but I'm still working on staying focused on a list. Those end cap sale items pique my interest from time to time. More than once I've returned home from what began as a speedy trip to the market with a new kitchen gadget, dog toy, or floral arrangement that I had no intention of buying. No matter how cute the thing was, I should have just left it in the store. Don't even get me started on those huge bulk discount warehouses. I can't even shop there anymore. My budget can't handle it, and I can never figure out where to put the fifty rolls of toilet paper when I get home. Bathroom storage cabinets just aren't big enough to hold those kinds of deals, so I do better settling for sales at the regular stores.

Aside from spur of the moment weaknesses, our goal is to get from point A to point B in the market with very little lingering along the way. Otherwise, our quick task of finding dinner ingredients turns into a bulging buggy of impulses. It's so hard! The minute we walk in and grab a cart, the marketing ploys begin. *Buy our stuff. Purchase this thing you really don't need. Look! Right here is the perfect product for you!* As we zigzag down each of the aisles, searching for the few things actually written on a list, the bombardment of great products captivates our minds, confuses our logic, and commandeers our pocketbooks. How do we survive? We make a list, check it twice, and stick with it. We don't buy all the extras. We avoid the lure of our impulsive desires.

At least we try.

Have you mastered this method of purchase? Me neither. But together, we could learn a lot about our spiritual lives as we reflect on the luring sales of consumer goods. See, just like our shopping focus, our goal in daily life should be to avoid caving in to unnecessary impulses in every area of life—even sin. If we focus on God's list for holy living, we are better equipped to walk right past the displays of earthly pleasures. We'll be ready to walk in the Spirit.

The Passage:

Re-read Galatians 5:16. Write down key points from the text and journal your thoughts about what you have read:

_____
_____
_____

The Details:

1. In your daily life, how do you walk in the Spirit? In what ways do you avoid the desires of the flesh by focusing on God?

_____
_____
_____

2. What are some solutions to getting out of a sinful situation—escaping the lust of the flesh, and living according to the Spirit?

_____
_____
_____

Prayer is a great way to get back on track with God. Our sin is not surprising to Him; nothing shocks God. He knows what we are going through, and He is waiting for us to call on Him for help. His desire is for us to walk in the Spirit, so if we ask for help in doing that, the Lord will be faithful to come to our aid.

4. Read Ephesians 2:1–3. Before we entered into relationship with Jesus Christ, were we able to walk in the Spirit? Why or why not? According to these verses, how did we live?

_____

VERSES WE KNOW BY HEART

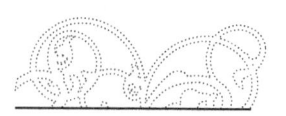

> "For the mind set on the flesh is death; but the mind set on the Spirit is life and peace" (Romans 8:6).

5. How does Romans 8:6–12 further describe this contrast between flesh and Spirit?

A Closer Look:

As we've discovered in a variety of ways through our study together, we are changed when we accept the gift of salvation. We are a new creation: no longer bound to the limits of this world and its wisdom, but free to live in light of eternity with assurance that God has given us salvation through faith in Jesus Christ. Making the decision to follow Jesus, and allow Him to be Lord of our lives, is much more than a one-time altar call experience. It's a lifetime of living out the faith we profess by making the right choices and living an obedient life according to the will of the Father.

We've broadened the idea with the concept of walking by the Spirit. Again, we're faced with choices and a need to focus, both of which require attention to one thing at a time. Try to add too many distractions and we lose our ability to concentrate. In our spiritual walk with the Lord, we are more obedient followers of Him, guided by His Spirit and moved by His will when we are completely focused. The things of the world will try to capture our attention, but as today's verse points out, we won't follow the flesh if we're walking in the Spirit.

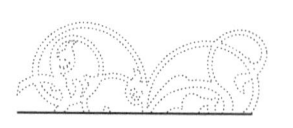

Submit your life to the Lordship of Jesus Christ!

A Question for Your Life Today:

Today, what area of your life needs to be submitted to the Lordship of Christ? What desires of the flesh are getting in the way of your spiritual growth? Describe:

I pray along with you that the Lord will free up these hindrances from your life, and that, through the power and mercy of the Holy Spirit, you will be able to walk in newness of life in that particular area of life.

DAY THREE

FLESH DRIVEN - GALATIANS 5:17–21

The Focus Verse:

For the flesh sets its desire against the Spirit, and the Spirit against the flesh; for these are in opposition to one another, so that you may not do the things that you please. **Galatians 5:17**

The Main Thought:

Don't let your flesh nature rule you.

The Story within the Story:

Occasionally, on a busy intersection in our city, we witness the phenomenon of peaceful protests. In one corner of the intersection stand the sign carrying protesters, announcing their views to the world on stark white poster-board signs sprinkled with marker-written slogans. No amount of artwork or clever phrases on the statements of angst will make their opinion logical, but because of the freedoms we enjoy in our country, they are allowed free expression of opinion.

On the adjacent corner, separated from the protesters by asphalt, traffic lights, and vehicles passing by, are the people who set up camp to protest the protesters. Waving flags and holding signs refuting the claims of the other group, these responders come out in greater number, and with much more zeal than the initiators. What is the opposition's motivation? What one side sees as a good idea the other side knows is nothing but hot air and earthly ideals. The two groups engage in peaceful banter and disagreement, setting their arguments up against each other, hoping to reel the commuters into their side of the fight. By the end of the afternoon, both groups pack

VERSES WE KNOW BY HEART

up their signs, folding lawn chairs and pride, and head back home.

Think about today's focus verse. The flesh sets itself up against the Spirit, and vice versa. When we are set on reacting in a godly way, the enemy is there shoving his cardboard excuses in our face. When we are tempted to follow the flesh, God sends His Spirit to convict us and draw us back to right living. The two are in a continuous tango in our minds. Which will we choose to follow today, right this moment?

The Passage:

Read Galatians 5:17–21. Write down key points from the text and journal your thoughts about what you have read:

_____

_____

_____

The Details:

1. In our focus verse today, Galatians 5:17, we see that the desires of the flesh and Spirit are set against each other. What do you think that means?

_____

_____

_____

**"Now the deeds of the flesh are evident . . ."
(Galatians 5:19a).**

2. How do sinful desires distract us from God?

_____

_____

_____

WEEK SIX

3. List the sins of the flesh as found in Galatians 5:19–21.

Which of these are you battling today, or in the past week?

4. Read Romans 7:1–25. What conflict does this passage describe?

5. According to verses 24–25, who helps Paul overcome the flesh and the law of sin?

The apostle Paul describes our inner struggle between sin and godliness in this passage. In verse 25 he acknowledges that it is Jesus who can help him with this dilemma.

6. Now read Romans 8:1–12. Who frees Paul, and us, from the bondages of sin? How? What new insight do you have about this passage that we first read yesterday?

Paul's focus is on the Lord, who frees him from the bondage of the desires of the flesh. I like this passage because of its clear articulation of the daily workings of the Christian life. When we become believers, the temptations and opportunities to sin don't go away; but as we give those things less focus in our lives, we will become more immune to their luring calls.

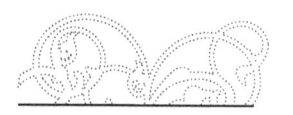

When we give the lures of sin less focus in our life, we will become more immune to their deceptive calls.

7. Write out a prayer that you might pray in the event that you were asking the Lord to keep you focused on desiring the Spirit:

___

___

___

A Closer Look:

Good intentions don't always win the day. We still fall short, every day, but God is faithful to forgive. As we repent of new sin and refocus our lives of walking in the Spirit, the flesh nature will be kept in check, and hopefully at bay.

It is interesting to note in today's focus passage that along with immorality, drunkenness, and sorcery are things like jealousy, envy, and strife. If we only focus on what we consider to be the biggest sins on the list, we will easily fall into the trap of pride, thinking we don't battle with any flesh issues. But look at this list! Even a little envy and jealousy leads us a long way down the road of sin. God wants us to be free from anything that would hold us back from a growing, thriving relationship with Him.

A Question for Your Life Today:

Have you experienced jealousy, or had someone become very jealous toward you? If left unresolved, what happens when jealousy takes root? How is that different from any other flesh issue?

___

___

___

Now that we've seen the dangers of jealousy, strife, and other sins, let's press on to the glorious blessings of walking in the ways of the Lord.

DAY FOUR

FRUIT DRIVEN - GALATIANS 5:22–23

The Focus Verse:

But the fruit of the Spirit is love, joy, peace, patience, kindness, goodness, faithfulness. **Galatians 5:22**

The Main Thought:

Cultivate the fruit of the Spirit.

The Story within the Story:

"Today, I'm definitely having a raisin kind of day," I announced as I plodded into my small group classroom one Tuesday morning.

"What on earth do you mean by that?" A friend said.

"I'm in such a bad mood that my fruit is drying up more and more by the minute. I just know I'm not showing any of the fruit of the Spirit in my life right now. My grapes are turning into raisins!" Giggles erupted across the room, but the seriousness of my mood couldn't be hidden behind a surface level smile.

That morning had been quite a challenge already. I'd gotten irritated by a few emails, the weather was bad, I was tired and just really not in the best mood. Deadlines were looming, and my to-do list was getting longer by the second. Everything may have looked fine on the outside, but inside I was a tangled-up mess of unhappiness.

VERSES WE KNOW BY HEART

Feeling the weight of the world on my shoulders and uttering the griping comments of a complainer in my spirit, I dumped my tote bag on the chair next to me and sunk into my seat. Prayer request sheets were passed around the class, and I didn't even bother to share my woes with the prayer team. All I wanted to do was have a pity party, yet I knew in doing so my fruit was withering like a raisin in the sun.

An hour later, after spending time in God's Word and hearing encouraging words from friends, I was in a totally different state of mind. Through fellowship with others and with God I felt renewed. My raisin-like emotions began filling back up with the equipping power of the Holy Spirit, and I was ready to face the world with patience and kindness. I felt peace and joy, and even a little love, for those who had frustrated me earlier in the day. Goodness, gentleness, and self-control were a possibility once again.

As we parted company for the day, I looked up at my precious friends and exclaimed, "I am officially a grape again. Thanks!"

The Passage:

Read Galatians 5:22–23. Write down key points from the text and journal your thoughts about what you have read:

_____

_____

_____

The Details:

1. List all the fruit of the Spirit, as revealed in Galatians 5:22–23:

_____

_____

_____

2. What is the first fruit of the Spirit listed? In light of last week's lesson on love, why do you think it is listed first?

_____

_____

_____

3. Who do you find most difficult to love? How can cultivating the fruit of the Spirit, such as a greater ability to love others, help you love these tough-to-love people?

_____

_____

_____

4. Which quality listed in Galatians 5:22–23 is the most difficult for you to display? Why?

_____

_____

_____

5. Verse 23 includes the statement, "against such things there is no law." Why is there no law against the fruit listed?

_____

_____

_____

There is no law against the outworking of the love of God! He is truthful, faithful, and perfect. When we work out our faith according to His precepts and ways, we are in line with His will. Being safely protected in the will of God keeps us on the narrow path of faith, and within His perfect law. Therefore, there is no law of God that is contrary to the ways of God!

VERSES WE KNOW BY HEART

A Closer Look:

Sitting in a restaurant this week, I watched my son try to drink liquid out of an empty glass. He kept slurping through the air-packed straw, in hopes that maybe he'd get one more drop out of the drink he'd been sipping. What made his actions so odd? Sitting about a foot away from the empty glass that was getting all his attention was a new, full, bubbling mug of soda. It was just sitting there waiting for him. The waiter brought it to the table, but the customer missed it. He didn't see it. Owen just didn't tap in to the resources available to him.

Likewise, we allow our fruit of the Spirit to dry up and become ineffective when we forget to tap into the unending power of God. God wants us to live lives full of His Spirit and to exhibit the godly qualities that reflect His nature. But we have to tap into it! If we settle for pity parties and raisin days, we'll miss out on all He has for us. We have to assess our situation, pray and seek the Lord in the moments we feel all dried up, and allow the Holy Spirit to revive us once again.

A Question for Your Life Today:

In what areas of your life are you experiencing a raisin kind of day? What can you do to overcome these issues?

_____

_____

_____

DAY FIVE

KEEP IN STEP WITH THE SPIRIT - GALATIANS 5:24–26

The Focus Verse:

If we live by the Spirit, let us also walk by the Spirit. **Galatians 5:25**

WEEK SIX

The Main Thought:

Follow God!

The Story within the Story:

The Apostle Paul taught the early church, and the church through the ages, how to live the Christian life. One of the things I find most powerful about his letters is the transparency of his testimony. Paul isn't afraid to talk about his weaknesses, his trials, or the ways he has learned to overcome adversity. We could learn a lot about authentic faith from the life of Paul.

In his letter to the church at Galatia, the apostle mentions how he has been crucified with Christ. Physically, he was not nailed to the cross next to Jesus that day at Calvary. So, what could he mean? Friend, through our relationship with Jesus Christ we are tied to Christ with much more than a simple "get out of jail free" card to place on our playing board of life. A genuine faith brings with it the experience of a life lived for our Savior. We have a commitment to the principles and precepts of Scripture and of obedience to the will of the Father. Like Paul, we too can feel as though we've "been crucified with Christ, and it is no longer I who live, but Christ who lives in me . . ." (Galatians 2:20).

Just as we've discovered before, our sin has been atoned for by the blood of Jesus's sacrifice. Also, that sacrifice is a hint of how we are to live an obedient life of faith, as we submit our best ideas, plans, and goals to God. He directs our paths, and leads us to the best possible life we could live. Most importantly, the Lord leads us to salvation.

His Spirit guides us into right living.

Godly living.

God-honoring living.

The Passage:

Read Galatians 5:24–26. Write down key points from the text and journal your thoughts about what you have read:

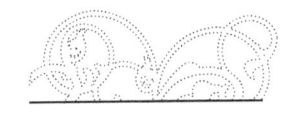

_____

_____

> **Jesus Christ means much more to us than a simple "get out of jail free" card to place on our playing board of life.**

VERSES WE KNOW BY HEART

_____

_____

_____

_____

The Details:

1. Read Galatians 2:20. What does Paul describe, and how does that relate to our determination to walk by the Spirit?

_____

_____

_____

Coming full circle—beginning and ending our week on the fruit of the Spirit with the concept of being crucified with Christ—helps us understand where we tap into the power and ability to function in the fruit of the Spirit. It isn't by our own effort or best intentions; it is only through our relationship with Jesus and our standing as children of God that we are equipped with the spiritual gifts and spiritual fruit.

2. Have you ever heard the phrase, "actions speak louder than words?" Looking at today's focus verse, how do our actions reflect our "living" by the Spirit and "walking" by the Spirit?

_____

_____

3. Another popular Christian phrase is "walking the walk." Walking is active, a working out of our faith, rather than talking, which focuses on words. In what ways do you personally *walk* out your Christian faith?

_____

_____

_____

WEEK SIX

4. What does 1 John 2:6 reveal about the relationship between following Jesus and walking the walk? What does this imply about the importance of obedience?

___

"Whoever claims to live in him must walk as Jesus did" (1 John 2:6, New International Version).

5. Galatians 5:26 includes a powerful admonishment as this passage closes. What does it warn us about? Why do you think this is the "last word" in our passage?

___

6. How would we become boastful in showing spiritual fruit in our lives? Is being busy, or legalistic, in our approach healthy? How could those issues lead to boastfulness?

___

Spiritual maturity involves genuine faith and authentic fruit, as well as servant hearts acting in humble, spiritually mature ways.

A Closer Look:

As we've gone through our study together, we've discovered that:

- Jesus' perfect sacrifice is the way to salvation, open to all who believe.
- We are saved by faith, not by our good works.
- Our relationship with Jesus Christ sustains us in suffering, strengthens us in weakness, and forgives us in our daily sins.
- God is all-powerful and faithful to carry us through the most difficult times.

VERSES WE KNOW BY HEART

- Our spiritual growth will reflect a working out of our beliefs that produces right reactions and servant hearts.

- If we are dedicated to loving others with the love of the Lord, we will shun selfishness and envy, and exhibit the selfless sacrifice of a true Christ follower.

- God is ultimately concerned with conforming us to His image through the process of sanctification.

- We are called to glorify God.

In this week's lesson, as we draw to a close, we now know that the loving foundation and gifts God has equipped us with will show forth through the fruit of the Spirit: not a system of works or good deeds, but a lifestyle of glorifying the Father, and obediently following His Son.

A Question for Your Life Today:

How will your life change if you apply the principles you've learned in this study?

_____

_____

_____

Take a moment to close this lesson in prayer, praising God for His Son, and your life in Him. Ask the Lord to use you in greater measure to impact the world with the truth of the gospel.

Thanks, friend, for finishing this study with excellence. I pray that you will continue on in your desire to grow closer to Jesus. Keep seeking the Lord through His Word!

Serving alongside you in His kingdom,

Jennifer

WORKS CITED:

Walvoord, John F.; Zuck, Roy B.; Dallas Theological Seminary: *The Bible Knowledge Commentary: An Exposition of the Scriptures*. Wheaton, IL: Victor Books, 1983–c1985, S. 2:537.

Note to Leaders

Visit **www.randallhouse.com** and receive a free Leader's Guide for *Verses We Know by Heart New Testament Edition*. Discover tools to aid you in leading your church or small study group through a six-week journey that will cultivate a deeper walk with God. In this on-line resource you will find teacher thoughts, quick questions, and suggested extras for each week. You will also find a personal letter from Jennifer Devlin.

To order additional copies of *Verses We Know by Heart* call
1-800-877-7030
or log onto
www.randallhouse.com.

Quantity discount for 24 or more copies at $8.99 each.

Another small group study from Jennifer Devlin

Verses We Know by Heart
Old Testament Edition
ISBN 9780892655656
$10.99

Order of 24 or more copies will have a quantity discount - $8.99 each

How To Grow Your Faith

Birds in My Mustard Tree
Susanne Scheppmann
$10.99—Group Pricing Available!
ISBN: 0892656689

Birds in My Mustard Tree is a small group study that looks at the subject of faith as an active, growing part of our walk with God. Faith may begin as a mustard seed, but the goal is to expand it until we have birds roosting on our mustard tree of faith.

God wants each of us to have an excited anticipation about who He is and how He works in our lives every day. The evidence of our growing faith also encourages others to trust God. This study begins with a review of the concept of faith that leads to lessons on exercising faith, amazing faith, shattered faith, resting in faith, and a stronger faith.

Lessons Learned from an Unlikely Leader

Walking With Moses—Talking With God
Cinda King
$10.99—Group Pricing Available!
ISBN: 0892656670

Walking With Moses—Talking With God is a small group study that will take students on a journey through the most significant events in the life of Moses as he finds himself leading the children of Israel. Situations lived by Moses will bring clarity to the path many others walk in following God; times of questioning, strange encounters, significant markers, and evidence of provision and protection. There are many lessons to be learned from the epic adventures in the life of Moses.

randall house

**To order call 1-800-877-7030
or visit www.randallhouse.com**

Mom's Love
D6 Devotional Magazines for Kids!

D6 Devotional Magazines are unique because they are the only brand of devotional magazines where the entire family studies the same Bible theme at the same time.

Think about how long it would take you to track down all of the resources for each member of your family to connect with God on the same topic. Who has that kind of time? We do! It's not that we have nothing else to do, we are just passionate about D6. So look no further, we have created the resource you are looking for, and it works!

D6 Devotional Magazines are full color, interactive, fun, and exciting tools to connect with God and with each other. Check it out!

To subscribe **800.877.7030** D6magazines.com

splink

Simple ways to **Link** your family together.

splink gives Dads and Moms simple ways to link their family together spiritually.

Sign-up online for **splink** and receive a FREE digital family resource each week!

It's FREE! D6Family.com

CPSIA information can be obtained
at www.ICGtesting.com
Printed in the USA
LVHW062240120322
712969LV00001B/1

9 780892 655540